HISTORY
OF THE
ENGLISH
HERB
GARDEN

HISTORY
OF THE
ENGLISH
HERB
GARDEN

KAY N. SANECKI

FOREWORD BY
ANTHONY HUXLEY

WARD LOCK

To my daughter Diana Irene

God send thee hartes ease . . . pray
God give thee but one handfull of
heavenly heartes ease, which passeth all
the pleasaunt flowers that grow in this Worlde.

Bullen's Bulwark of Defence *(1562)*

First paperback edition 1994

First published 1992 by Ward Lock
Villiers House, 41/47 Strand, London WC2N 5JE

A Cassell Imprint

Typeset by Litho Link Ltd, Welshpool, Powys

Printed and bound in Hong Kong by Dah Hua Printing Press Co. Ltd.

Cataloguing in Publication Data for this title
is available from the British Library

ISBN 0-7063-7233-6

CONTENTS

Author's Acknowledgements

I am grateful to innumerable colleagues who have contributed to my ideas. First, every garden or plant historian takes for granted access to Tusser, Gerard, Parkinson and tribes of nurserymen and amateur gardeners whose records remain. It is time they were thanked for the cornerstones upon which we base our own opinions. Among my supporters I must acknowledge help and time given generously by the librarians and their staff of the Lindley Library, Royal Horticultural Society, The Royal Pharmaceutical Society and The Royal Botanic Gardens Kew, who over the years have nurtured my knowledge. To the staff of County Records Offices of Dorset, Essex, Oxfordshire and Somerset, my thanks. Colleagues and friends who have responded readily during the preparation of this book and to whom I am indebted include: Muriel Arber, Jane Brown, Tom Dor, Kathie Down, the late Monica Dunbar, Ruth Duthie, Lady Hanham, Dr John Harvey, Simon and Judith Hopkinson, Rosie Humphreys, Barbara Keen, Anthony Lyman-Dixon, Pippa Rakusen, Hazel le Rougetel, Prue Scurfield, and Alison Taylor of the Hitchin Museum. My sincere thanks are due to The Marchioness of Salisbury and The Royal Horticultural Society for permission to publish their plant lists.

Publishers Acknowledgements

The publishers are grateful to the following persons, libraries, and institutions for granting permission to reproduce the following illustrations: the author (pp. 18, 20, 23, 24, 25, 27, 34, 44, 46, 51, 53, 54, 59, 62, 71, 73, 82, 83, 87, 88, 89, 93, 96, 98, 99 & 102); Michael H. Ransom (p. 76); H.P. Mason (p. 122); Iris Hardwick Library (pp. 74, 106, 107, 110, 111, 115, 118 & 119); Victoria and Albert Museum (pp. 10 & 11); Trinity College Library, Cambridge (p. 14); the Mansell Collection (p. 16); Somerset Record Office (p. 49); The Royal Society (p. 63); Chelsea Physic Garden (p. 69); Hitchin Museum (p. 77); The Bach Centre (p. 91); the Knebworth Estates (pp. 84 & 85); the Knole Estates (p. 97); and *The Times* (p. 102).

The coloured illustrations on pp. 98 & 99 are also reproduced by kind permission of Mr Ronald Brownlow and acknowledgement is made to the Medici Society in the reproduction of the colour illustrations on p. 102. The photograph on p. 95 was taken by Bob Challinor.

The woodcuts are taken from *Rariorum plantarum historia* (Leyden, 1601), written by one of the most eminent plantsman and scholar of the time, Carolus Clusius (Charles de l'Écluse). His herbal included numerous economic plants in addition to herbs, and the woodcuts are remarkable for their botanical accuracy for that period. The work is regarded generally as a reference point for the modern knowledge for genera, upon which Linneaus built.

FOREWORD

I F one starts to think about it, it is amazing that primitive people ever added plants to their diet. So many plants are unpalatable, and not a few actively toxic. There must have been many traumatic trials and errors as people assessed plant possibilities. The value of certain plants in ill-health obviously emerged from this long-drawn-out sampling, eventually providing amazingly detailed knowledge of their attributes.

The power of plants in all manner of healing, providing strength, inducing sleep, calming tension, creating hallucinations, let alone killing, led to their being considered magical and the property of whatever spirits or deities were locally believed in. Hence such plants became the special province of shamans, medicine men and witch doctors, and their attributes became wrapped up within rituals and myths to enhance the power of the shamans and hide the knowledge from ordinary mortals.

The people of the British Isles were late on this scene, if only because their own arrival was so much delayed by Ice Ages. The precepts and superstitions of their European forebears were later overlaid with the knowledge and beliefs of the Romans, who in turn brought their knowledge from classical, Biblical and other civilizations with which they had contact. When British herbalism emerged in its own right in the so-called Dark Ages, it was compounded of both factual and superstitious information. Many plants were regarded as potent for good or evil, according to the way they were used by witches, quite apart from any medicinal properties they might have. The herbalists who understood the true worth of these plants became an important part of the community.

The term 'herbs' came to embrace medicinal uses, 'pot-herbs' as flavourings for food (so often dull or unsavoury), and household and personal sweeteners. Much unfounded belief crept into medical herbalism, yet there was always a nucleus of real value in many of the plants concerned, and this has been immensely reinforced by scientific appraisal in this century. A great many people in the British Isles grow herbs, mainly perhaps for the kitchen, and also for dyeing, but in some cases for tonic and more specific healing qualities. When mainstream medicine seems not to help, people turn increasingly to herbal remedies.

In this book Kay Sanecki spells out this history in the British scene: she describes the beginnings of herbalism, the many uses of herbal plants, the major herbalists and their often great books, and brings matters right up to date, spelling out the doubtless inevitable commercialization of herbal products, which are now big business in industrial herbalism; their recognition in the British Pharmacopoeia (which includes products from around 80 plant genera today); the production of modern herbal books (to which she has previously contributed herself), with biographies of authors and herb growers; and finally describes the resurgence of herb gardens, many though not all modelled on past exemplars. After their almost total eclipse during the last century, herb gardens are today an important feature of many gardens large and small, and always seem a magnet to visitors.

Much of the research into more recent herbal history is entirely original and from unpublished sources, and many of the fascinating illustrations have not been reproduced before. The result is a unique work which will surely become the most important source-book on British herbal history.

Anthony Huxley

PREFACE

To trace the story of those plants we call herbs is to unlock the history of flowering plants themselves. They emerge from a nebulous past as being already very important in the Biblical and classical worlds. They are a subject of the earliest manuscripts and drawings and have names that link them to the banners of the Gods.

To the Anglo-Saxons in England herbs were vital components of everyday life, even ensuring protection from the terrifying unknown. In the medieval world they were endowed with the symbolisms of Christendom; to the Tudors they became playthings: indoors for the enhancement of person and habitation, outdoors to form playful patterns on the ground. Once men's minds were occupied by mechanical progress and sophistication on the home front and exotic plant hunting elsewhere, herbs were relegated to the old woman's parlour and back street shop and were maintained as mere denizens of the kitchen garden.

A century ago these plants, whose essential oils have served man's multiple requirements, as antiseptic, demulcent, stimulant, anaesthetic, tranquillizer or sweetener, were superseded by synthetic drugs and perfumery. Their economic importance waned. As many drugs have proved to have unacceptable side effects, older plant wisdom is being reassessed and new discoveries pursued, motivated by a renewed awareness of the natural world.

Attendant upon this loss of role as garden plants, the Edwardians vested herbs only with quaint and legendary interest. Before World War I, herbs were merely traditional plants, at the nadir of their existence. Some were sought in the countryside by amateur botanists and wild flower enthusiasts and were written about with emphasis upon their country names and folk lore. Few were cultivated.

Decorative herb gardens of the mid and late twentieth century are by no means living museums, but a manifestation of our preoccupation with heritage. Whereas pretend medieval markets, Victorian kitchens, restored forges and steam engines satisfy nostalgia and emphasize a sense of loss, herb gardens today represent old plants in new gardens. The traditions remain; the settings are new.

Where then do we search for historical reference for the formal decorative herb garden so popular in contemporary garden design? Given an area of garden we feel impelled to inscribe some form of pattern upon it; but what suggests the approach? Herb borders set in the age-old traditions of cottage gardens and meadow banks beg no question, but the geometric arrangement of beds, the central feature, the level site, require a deeper investigation. Some would argue that there has to be a certain rusting over of the pages of garden history, that imitative ideas are too ephemeral, or in this instance, that the plants themselves represent the true continuum because they have not changed over the centuries. Whether or not the conclusions I have reached are valid, only a wider public can assess.

K.N.S.

I

GARDEN OF MIRACLES
(to 1500)

ROMAN BRITAIN

When we claim that during the waning millenium man has perfected the art of taming the land and has developed the science of horticulture, we overlook the highly civilized Roman culture which flourished in England for four centuries from the first century AD. Gardening for pleasure is a manifestation of civilization and evidence is apparent of 'pleasure gardens' as part of Roman habitation, most notably at Fishbourne Palace, near Chichester, W. Sussex. Many familiar fruits and vegetables were introduced into Britain at the time of the Roman occupation, via trade or travellers. While many plants fell out of cultivation afterwards, some continued to be grown and increasingly so by the early Christian communities of monks. The vine which had been introduced by the Romans was one of them: the Venerable Bede confirmed that vines constituted an important crop by the eighth century.

We cannot help wondering just how many plants arrived during that period. Some authorities claim the number to be as high as 400, but with considerable certainty, the list includes several well-known herbs: lavender, dill, rosemary, chervil, hyssop, alexanders, valerian, rue, coriander, sage and lavender cotton were among them. Some, such as valerian and the unloved ground elder, naturalized readily and have been part of our flora ever since, but others, lavender for example, must soon have fallen out of general cultivation and it is considered to have been reintroduced about the year 1200. Other plants from the native northern European flora would have been deemed worthy of a place and taken into gardens, such as mallow, marjoram, St John's wort and foxglove. Flowers attractive to bees would have been grown also, more possibly in a small *hortus* away from the leisure areas of the villa because honey was not only the major sweetener of food, but was employed extensively as a preservative and in numerous medicinal preparations.

Other important plants which reached our shores at the time were the fig (*Ficus carica*), walnut (*Juglans regia*), medlar (*Mespilus germanica*), mulberry (*Morus nigra*), cherries and little plums (*Prunus* spp:), cabbages, nettles eaten as a vegetable, carrots, parsley, asparagus, peas, lettuce, turnip and marrow. Above all, favourite flowers included the lily, rose, acanthus and apparently a form of pansy. Not only in England, but all over Europe the art of gardening was eclipsed by the fall of the Roman Empire and the few hundred years that followed in England have been well named indeed — the Dark Ages.

Roman medicine

The remedies used by the Romans were essentially herbal. The restorative properties of henbane, wormwood, belladonna and opium were known along with other vegetable drugs and because knowledge centred upon Mediterranean plants, a need was created for some of them to be imported. At the same time powers from the gods were invoked, incantations and a soupçon of magic were accepted rituals of healing. Healing by mortal man was accepted as impossible, the Classical culture had depended upon the gods for help and the early Christian Romans maintained that a Christian God could do all and more that pagan gods could achieve. Thus healing became part and parcel of prayer and penance; disease purified the soul. Early Christian communities continued to serve the sick after the fall of the great Roman Empire, relating ailments and afflictions to the various saints, who replaced the ancient gods.

Meanwhile, back at base as it were, herbal treatises continued to be written about plants known in the Mediterranean. Of supreme importance was *De Materia Medica*, a five-volume tome by Pedanius Dioscorides, a Greek serving as a military physician with the Roman legions. Over 600 plants, 35 animal products and 90 minerals are described in *De Materia Medica* which proved to be the basis of pharmaceutical knowledge and writing for centuries to come. Much of his work was translated into Arabic around the ninth century and there are some Anglo-Saxon versions.

The four humours

Galen was another Greek doctor working in Rome in the first century AD and in many ways his theories complemented the knowledge of Dioscorides. Galen adhered to the teaching of Hippocrates (popularly known as the Father of Medicine), eschewing magic and ritual, and concerned himself with environmental treatment. Today such an approach is widely fashionable, but to Hippocrates it meant merely considering 'the whole person' in a theory that attributed illness to an imbalance of 'humours'. The four humours were blood, phlegm, black bile and yellow bile. To these Galen extended his own theories, involving the four natural elements of fire, earth, air and water, which reflected the humours to produce types of people or temperaments: the sanguine or buoyant, the phlegmatic, bilious or sluggish, the melancholic or dejected, and the choleric or quick-tempered man. Further, he involved four more qualities of heat, moisture, dryness and cold to describe and categorize human disorders.

He admitted that a person may perhaps not fit precisely into these categories: his excuse was that a man may have a 'type' peculiar to himself; thus idiosyncratic. Then, he argued, that the differences between types indicated a predisposition to certain disease. Over the years it is understandable that an overlay of astrology provided as many answers as it confounded, either in the planetary ruler of a healing plant or of an area of the human anatomy. A general acceptance of Galen's beliefs inhibited the progress of rational medicine and the true nature of infection for a very long time. Nevertheless, we must not lose sight of the fact that it was the herbs, whether used properly or not, that constituted the bulk of his *Materia Medica*.

CHRISTIAN COMMUNITIES

This muddle of ideas was safeguarded by the Christians in the monastic communities. The monks saw their role in the care of the sick and aged as a Christian duty. It takes but a modicum of imagination to visualize pilgrims, the tourists of the age, travelling to their distant chosen shrine, resting at the monasteries and relating common remedies and topical ideas in their evening chatter. Much of this knowledge was not only practised but safeguarded as literature within monastic cloisters.

In England after the departure of the Romans, paganism drove out Christianity for a time, although it remained in Welsh monasteries, now commemorated by place names beginning with *Llan*. Following St Augustine's reintroduction of Christianity in his great settlement of Canterbury in Kent, English monasteries became renowned for their learning, threatened only by marauding Danes. Beyond their walls, folklore, ritual and incantation became a mish-mash of ideas practised by herb women, travelling bone-setters and soothsayers. Evidence from those early centuries is flimsy and it is from a Continental monastery that we have a pleasant description of what a monk was growing in his garden.

A monk describes his garden

Despite the Bavarian location of his plot we can share his enjoyment for the same plants were cultivated in England at that time. A talent for composing Latin verse developed early in the life of Walahfrid Strabo, a monk and later Abbot at Abbey Reichenai in the ninth century. His manuscript lay forgotten until *c.* 1509, since when delightful translations have been made of *Hortulus* (a little garden). The verses enumerate in an appealingly simple way the herbs he grew in his garden, and his enthusiasm and enjoyment shine through.

First he records the seasons: 'Winter, image of age, who like a great belly Eats up the whole year's substance and heartlessly Swallows the fruits of our unstinted labour'. Having set the year as his backdrop, the herbs he describes include: sage,

Pliny the Elder wrote Historia Naturalis *in the first century* AD. *It was of monumental proportion and during the Medieval period copies were made and sumptuous illustrations added.*

southernwood, wormwood and horehound ('If ever A vicious stepmother mixes in your drink Subtle poisons, or makes a treacherous dish of lethal aconite for you, don't waste a moment Take a dose of wholesome horehound, that will counteract the damage you suspect'); then fennel ('what is more your rasping cough Will go if you take fennel-root mixed with wine'). He continues with iris, lovage and chervil: ('Now chervil, though it splits and divides itself In flimsy branches and gives but a paltry seed In its thick clusters of ears, yet flourishing All the year through gives largess to the poor And comfort'). Further references follow on lily and poppy ('Under the broad mantle of a single skin it holds A mass of seeds of remarkable power') clary, mint ('But if any man can name The full list of all the kinds and all the properties Of mint, he must be one who knows how many fish Swim in the Ocean, how many sparks Vulcan Sees fly in the air from his vast furnace in Etna'); pennyroyal, celery, betony, agrimony ('And here in handsome rows you see my agrimony. It clothes all the fields with its profusion; it grows wild in the woodland shade. Much honour it has and many Virtues — among them this: If it's crushed and drunk The draught will check the most violent stomach ache. And if an enemy blade happens to wound us We recommend to try its aid; pounding The shoots and putting them on the open place'); tansy, catmint, radish, rose, ('It well deserves its name of Flower of Flowers) and lily ('Over against it grows the famous lily Its flowers breathe a scent which hangs Long on the air; but he who crushes the gleaming buds Of its snow-white flowers will find to his amazement That the heavenly perfume sweet as a scattering nectar Vanishes in a moment. For in this flower Shines Chastity, strong in the sacred honour. If no unclean hand disturbs her, if No illicit passion does violence to her, The flower smells sweetly. But should her pride of innocence Be lost, the scent turns foul and noisome. These two flowers So loved and widely honoured, Have throughout the ages stood as symbols Of the Church's greatest treasures for it plucks the rose In token of blood shed by the Blessed Martyrs; the lily it wears as a shining sign of faith').

Thus we sense his intimacy with plants, a quality that shines through over the centuries because the herbs in our gardens are the very ones that he knew over a thousand years ago; here also is an early revelation of the esteem in which the rose and the lily were held as Christian symbols.

Pliny said 'Many simples, though their properties have been discovered, still lack names'. In the apothecary's enclosed garden the servant is instructed in the management of the still.

THE ARABIC INFLUENCE

In contrast, a sophisticated newly advancing Arabic culture was promoting 'scientific' knowledge of medicine, garnering herbal lore from Persia, India, Ancient China as well as Ancient Egypt and the Classical world. A cosmopolitan medical school at Solerno near Naples in Italy, and another at Montpellier in France represented the centres of medical knowledge. Arab physicians such as Rhazes and Avicenna led the field in enlightened writing derived from the best of accumulated knowledge, but the blind esteem in which Galen was still held, stifled medical advance by its own assumptions.

By the millenium the School at Solerno reached its peak; the Christian Church was something of a shambles and although it was the Arab world that preserved the traditions of *Materia Medica* and medical learning fresh ideas were emerging in northern Europe.

THE ENGLISH WAY

Anglo-Saxon 'scholarship' was well advanced when towards the end of the ninth century, Alfred of Wessex, commemorated as Alfred the Great, established a Court School and harnessed teachers from abroad, together with medical writings from the Arab world. Such traditions, augmented by local tradition was brought together in the *Leech Book of Bald*, compiled between 900 and 950 AD. Another remarkable manuscript is the *Lacunga*, generally considered to be a later eleventh-century compilation, set in verse.

Anglo-Saxon herbals

Many Anglo-Saxon manuscripts must have been disposed of at the time of the Norman Conquest, if only because they were written in a language incomprehensible to the conquerors. Anglo-Saxon libraries, which included medical works, were worthily praised at the time and remarkably, the leech books were written in the vernacular. Classical world herbals were copied and amended concerning plants indigenous to those countries, but experience and observations were added. Moreover, Christian monks as early as the eighth century begged their Continental counterparts to acquire for them some of the plants about which the ancient herbals had been written.

Leech Book of Bald

Oldest among these Anglo-Saxon manuscripts to survive is the *Leech Book of Bald*, now in the British Library, London, and considered to be the earliest medical treatise of Western Europe. It is of relevance here because in it herbs are named and their uses described. Penned on stout vellum, it was compiled under the direction of one Bald, by a scribe named Cild. 'Bald is the owner of this book which he ordered Cild to write', we learn from an epilogue verse. While six or seven centuries later herbals supported topical comment and some enlightened knowledge, early manuscripts such as the *Leech Book*, while not devoid of contemporary comment, recorded old heathen superstitions and a primitive herb lore and mythology handed down from some hoary antiquity.

Lacunga

Of much the same period as the various volumes of the *Leech Book*, is the herbal known as the *Lacunga* (also in the British Library), another ancient source of information about Anglo-Saxon medicine coupled with herbal lore. Perhaps one quote will suffice: 'To preserve swine from sudden death take the worts (herbs) lupin, bishopwort, hassock grass, tufty thorn, vipers bugloss, drive the swine to the fold, hang the worts upon the four sides and upon the door'. Implicit faith in the power of plants, against the unpredictable horrors of the unknown, is evident, and in order to assist the powers, rituals surrounded the gathering of the herbs. Sometimes the ground from which they had been collected was appeased, or thanked (we cannot be sure which!) with gifts of honey.

A third manuscript probably dating from the early twelfth century, and one which has excited research, is an illustrated copy of a Greek herbal and in England known as the

Herbal of Apuleius. Anglo-Saxon in origin, this particular copy now in the Bodleian Library, Oxford, was written at the Abbey of Bury St Edmunds, Suffolk. What makes it unique is that some of the plants are illustrated in a far more naturalistic way than was habitual in that period. The accepted theory is that some artist-naturalist illustrated from life a few of the plants he could identify to his own satisfaction, and copied the rest in the naïve manner of the day.

Anglo-Saxon herbal lore

The first two herbals in particular portray the traditional herb lore and belief in the terrifying unknown. All healing plants were overlaid by the mist of magic, an association which emanated from the Classical world's culture where the gods were omnipotent. Such beliefs emerged as pagan rites. Far more real were the vast forests, heaths and endless marshes believed to be populated by a host of supernatural creatures. Not only were there imaginary serpents, dragons and giants waiting to be slain, but myriads of fairies, elves, hobgoblins, devils, and brooding, stalking figures of lonely places, like pixies, trolls as well as witches, who knew how to fly to the moon! Perhaps modern technology has stamped out such bunkum, in some ways, and yet gremlins and viruses play a similar role today! This then was the period from which modern plant folk lore stems, the period in which ordinary people, as well as kings and warriors had only the plants of the field to treat their ailments, both physical and mental: while they accepted that they did not know why the plants healed, or why the plants afforded the power of protection, it was all part and parcel of the greatly-to-be-respected unknown. Ailments represented demonic possession, and some antidotal plant had to be found. Furthermore, the attendant gathering rituals had to be observed, many of which predated the Romans. Disease, it was claimed, could be banished by charming it away from the victim or by transferrring it to an inanimate object such as a rock or even flinging it into running water. Such ideas persisted for centuries, framed by ritual and folklore.

Of these beliefs, elf-shot or elf-disease loomed large, and disease, infection, and disabilities as well as misfortunes were ascribed to the mischievousness of elves — as unseen as Cupid's dart today! Malicious elves could attack horses and cattle, and an instruction for dealing with that ran: '. . . take sorrel-seed or Scotch wax, let a man sing Masses over it and put holy water on the horse or on whatsoever meat it be; have worts always with thee. For the same take the eye of a broken needle and give the horse a prick with it, no harm shall com.' As closely allied to unpredictable misfortunes was that of flying venom, comparable to infectious disease today. For that the magical nine herbs charm was chanted from which we gain the merest squint into the Anglo-Saxon philosophy.

The nine herbs lay

Part of the *Lacunga* comprises a celebrated extract of great Anglo-Saxon charm which sings of the nine herbs sacred to the god, Woden. Written in a Wessex dialect and believed to stem from the eleventh century, it no doubt represented a rendering of an earlier even primitive appeal. Translated by the Rev. Thomas Oswald Cockayne in his book *Leechdoms, Wortcunning and Starcraft of Early England* (1886), a rendering of a portion of it is given on the right.

What wondrous all-powerful herbs can these be? *Mugwort*, which for the Anglo-Saxons carried tremendous powers of protection; *waybroad*, which was later changed to plantain in the sixteenth century; *stime*, a cool descriptive name for watercress; *maythen* which has become chamomile; chervil; fennel; crab apple; *wergulu*, an appropriately fierce name for nettle; and the unidentified *atterlothe*.

MONASTERY GARDENS

Apart from the Roman period and scant monastic records little conclusive evidence exists of gardens in England before 1000 AD but following the arrival of the Normans, vague descriptions of monastic gardens emerge from the closing years of the eleventh century. Much of England existed in a state of considerable unrest although the religious

Now these nine worts have power
against nine magic outcasts
against nine venoms
and against nine flying vile things
and against the loathed things
that over land rove.
Against the red venoms
against the stinking venom
against the white venom
against the blue venom
against the yellow venom
against the green venom
against the dusky venom
against the brown venom
against the purple venom
Against worm blister
against water blister
against thorn blister
against thistle blister
against ice blister
Against venom blister

If any venom come
flying from east
or any come from north
or any from the south
or any from the west
over mankind
I alone know a running river
and nine serpents behold (him)
All weeds must
now worts give way
Seas may dissolve
and all salt water
When I this venom
from thee blow.

re : lt naffre recueta . Efa uor

An early illustrated manuscript depicts monks preparing medicines.

orders, with their close associations with the Continental mainland, provided peaceful havens in which the arts developed, including that of gardening. The gardens were invariably vineyards, orchards, and what today would be classed as a kitchen garden from which the whole community was provided with herbs and vegetables 'in season'. In addition to the main gardens there may have been several others: the Sacrist's garden supplied flowers for the decoration of the chapel or the adornment of the clergy, and sweet scented plants to provide incense when burned; the *Infirmarian* or infirmary garden — the physic garden — provided medicinal plants for the treatment of the sick. Plants grown specially for such virtues gained their horticultural suffix *officinale*.

The earliest record of a monastery garden in England is shown in a plan from Canterbury of 1165 showing herbarium, vineyard, orchard and fishponds. Considerable evidence is forthcoming that quiet secluded or enclosed gardens existed also purely for the refreshment of the soul or for philosophical meditation. At Winchester in southern England for example, a garden set aside was called 'Paradise'; and the garden within the confines of the cloister, the garth, in several abbeys was 'designed' for contemplation with the symbolic fount of life represented by water at the centre. Often also there were small privy gardens for the high officials (perpetuated in the Bishop's gardens in town-enfolded cathedrals today).

Prior to the Norman Conquest, monastic settlements numbered about thirty-five, located mainly in the Fens and the south-eastern counties. All were Benedictine. Canterbury established in 597 AD was the first, and other major foundations were at Ely, Peterborough, Bury St Edmunds, Romsey, Winchester and Abingdon. Convents and nunneries were few: at the time of the Conquest, nine were recorded. It was to the garden of the convent at Romsey that William Rufus and his companions were admitted 'as if to look at the roses and other flowering herbs', when in fact he wished to see Edile of Scotland, heiress to the Saxon line. Between the period 1066–1200, about 300 monasteries were established; new Orders came, bringing with them a European culture and a wider knowledge of the virtues of plants.

Various lists of plants cultivated in such monastic plots suggest a far less limited range than might be supposed. It is highly probable that a famous list of plants to be cultivated proclaimed by the great Charlemagne, ruler of the greater part of modern Europe, was plagiarized. This list headed by the Madonna lily and roses must have at least constituted the 'wants' list of the gardening monks, who were in a position to receive and exchange plant material, be it cuttings or roots, with travelling visitors. As John Harvey has pointed out there are one or two surprising omissions from the list of plants already known in cultivation such as the violet, hyssop and lemon balm.

Herbes

Allowing for doubtful identities, we base our ideas of monastic gardening upon various contemporary lists of plants. Of the flowers, roses, lilies and irises were of primary interest and fruit such as apples, pears, plums, cherries, vines, peaches, medlars, mulberries, and figs together with walnuts, hazel and chestnuts were grown. As was to be the custom until the seventeenth and eighteenth centuries, vegetables as we know them, were included as 'herbes' and lacked the variety and popularity of the modern-day diet. The list includes cucumber, melon, lettuce, rocket, cress, parsley, celery, chives, radish, chervil, some beans and peas, endive, mints, catmint, mallow, colewort, kohl-rabi, sweet bay, chicory, parsnip, carrot, various onion types, garlic, chicory and savory. Flax would have been grown probably extensively for the making of cloth and teazel with which to card wool and soapwort for washing were all included. Thus the gardens could have been stocked with a rich selection of plants and some additional ones, such as box and holly introduced from the countryside, especially if not readily available in the immediate locality.

Alexander Neckham (or Necham), one time head of the Abbey School at Dunstable, Bedfordshire, and after missions abroad Abbot of Cirencester at the turn of the thirteenth century, wrote extensively about his travels and his plants. From parts of his *De Naturis Rerum* we capture the delight of his ideal peaceful garden adorned with roses, lilies, heliotrope, violets and mandrake 'There you should have parsley, cost, fennel, southernwood, coriander, sage, savoy, hyssop, mint, rue, ditanny, smallage, pellitory, lettuce, garden cress and peonies . . . and pottage herbs such as beets, herb mercury, orach, sorrel and mallows'. For flavouring, anise, mustard and absynth were desirable and as physic plants, saffron, pennyroyal, borage and thyme.

Monks were the skilled cultivators, the perpetrators and exponents of gardening practice and their regulated peaceful existence allowed every opportunity to develop crops and viticulture, beekeeping, fish farming and fruit growing. Such husbandry was often on a large scale, for the monasteries were not only important land owners in the Middle Ages, but supported large communities in the buildings that clustered about the abbeys.

Herb gardens

Monastic gardens, and to a slightly lesser extent the enclosed gardens within castle precincts probably provide the salient starting point in the story of the development of our herb gardens. Every plant not listed as a fruit tree was considered to be a herb. If, like the rose, in addition to culinary or medicinal use it was of aesthetic value, that simply added to the charm. Apart from the orchard and nut walks, plants were cultivated in small regularly placed rectangular beds, each containing a single kind of plant. Thus a form of intensive cultivation could be continued, as one crop was cleared the space was available for another. Small beds allowed work to be carried on without the plants being disturbed or trodden upon and the ample paths between the rows of beds were of gravel or sand. The beds were probably outlined by boards of wood a few inches high, or stones sometimes traced the outline, so that the soil was slightly raised and could be built up. Such a simple layout persisted over several centuries of gardening and threads of the same idea, and indeed ideals, are woven into the kitchen gardens of

the modern period. Today the 'plant and pave' style or 'chequerboard' planting adopted by herb garden designers relates directly to this medieval reference.

Work rather than pleasure was represented in those utilitarian gardens and where the more austere Christian teaching disdained flowers as some Pagan frivolity, the monks endowed the blossoms with symbolic Christian meaning. Roses and lilies were the important devotional flowers of the Middle Ages, and the original meaning of rosary (or rosarie) is that of a rose garden enclosed for devotion.

Many herbs grown in medieval days were useful in medicine and cooking alike; some were even decorative, almost all were fragrant. Today the plants grown in herb gardens are little different from those known to medieval man, old plants in new gardens. Other denizens of the herb gardens of those far off days were many of the wild flowers of the countryside. Some of these were held in high regard and would be brought into the garden — or allowed to seed there — in order to have them to hand. Certainly corn marigold, ground ivy, agrimony, adder's tongue, celandine, yarrow, cowslip, primrose, wood sage and other north European native plants all smudged the garden boundary.

CASTLE GARDENS

Manuscripts were copied and recopied, contemporary illustrations were added. Herbs are being dug up (L) and made into medicine. (From a twelfth-century copy in Eton College Library.)

During this period following the Norman settlement, the high society of England was strongly international; royalty, ecclesiastical men, noblemen, and knights forged links of marriage and of learning with European countries. Thus the expansion of knowledge and the exchange of news established an informed and thinking culture among such classes. As far as gardens were concerned this manifested itself within monastic houses as a garden, beautiful and refreshing, made for contemplation in addition to the other gardens. Within the castle precincts, where space was at a premium, a garden was for

refreshment and repose so both garden and the plants within it became strongly symbolic. Not all castles had these little secluded gardens; Dover Castle on the cliffs of Kent, for example, was wholly a fortress.

Outside the castle walls were orchards and vineyards, but within, the gardens were for pleasure, not supply. At Winchester by the late twelfth century, there was a herber for the Queen and an aviary for the King's birds and there are not infrequent allusions, both in manuscripts and paintings, to gardens within the castle precincts, especially created for the ladies to enjoy.

Privacy in the castles must have been hard to achieve so a garden was a private place, a place for trysts. Such cloistered gardens are described sometimes as herbarium or 'herber' and would probably be turved, obviously as a lawn, and planted with flowers, daisies, violets and periwinkles, to form a flowery mead. Other smaller gardens were made perhaps as a ladies' walk, or 'allure' on top of the ramparts, or at the summit of a tower. 'Gloriette' is the name given to the vantage points of towers high up above the castle, an architectural term which signifies 'joy'. Here safe from assault and in privacy, small roof gardens or *Hortus Conclusus* were made. In contemporary symbolism, these tiny plots sometimes walled or fenced about, together with those that developed between the clustered buildings of manorial estates were an emblem of the Virgin Mary's virginity. Here flowers specially sacred to Mary flourished: the Madonna lily (*Lilium candidum*) emblem of her purity and faith; the rose, perfectly symmetrical and before the mid-thirteenth century associated with Christ's perfection; and the purple iris (*Iris germanica*), a symbol of the immaculate conception, and the violet (*Viola odorata*) for humility.

The flowery mead

A Dominican monk Albert Magnus worked on a treatise on gardening (c. 1260) and explained how to make a flowery mead (a meadow of flowers). The plot was to be covered with good turf, well beaten down and then planted with sweet-smelling herbs like rue, and basil and sage and flowers such as violets, columbines and lilies. Plants were not set in beds or rows, but lavishly dotted about so that there would be no distinction between this and the fields and glades of the countryside. These were the self-same flowers, simple and uncultivated, and were brought in from the fields to create the flower-filled meadow.

THE PARADISE GARDEN

Medieval man was consumed by thoughts of his relationship with God. The earthly journey was fraught with problems, and the ultimate perfection would be Heaven. In a garden he was transported in spirit, uplifted by the song of birds, the wonder of the scent and colour of the flowers and the bounty they represented. Plants were loved and believed in and all these plants were herbs; they were valued not only for their beauty or delicacy of form but for their service to man. Such gardens are represented in Medieval paintings as plots quartered by paths, of sand or gravel, or they appear as flowery mead, the turf sprinkled with flowers (herbs), often with seats of turf or fragrant chamomile around, suggesting rest and enjoyment and perhaps a conduit, fountain or trough of water. This represented the fount of life and invariably formed the central feature in the cloister gardens of the monasteries and abbeys where many of these symbolic flowers were cultivated also. The monks allied less to the erotic connotations of the 'paradise' garden than did the continental travellers, the returning Crusaders in particular, influenced by the notion of courtly love.

However those early gardens are considered today, the fact remains that a garden came to represent pleasure, home and an escape from the outside world. It is from the gardens of this period that reference comes for shady arbours and flowery mead which inspired the *fleuri à mille fleurs* background to Medieval tapestries. In much the same way that flowers speckled the turf of gardens, the same flowers could fill the groundwork of the tapestries: violets, daisies, cyclamen, marigold and lily-of-the-valley, ragged robin, snowflake, columbine, scarlet pimpernel, feverfew, clary sage, periwinkle and pinks.

JOHN OF GADDESDEN

In England the first major work on botanical medicine was a manuscript prepared by a doctor-cleric at Oxford: John of Gaddesden. Probably written between 1314–17, the work was entitled *Rosa Medicine* (although it became known as *Rosa Angelica*) because like the rose, the book was compiled in five parts and it excelled all other treatises on medicine 'as the rose excels all flowers'. The work was an acknowledged rendering from Greek, Arabic and Jewish sources, combined with eleventh- and twelfth-century writing together with contemporary observations. 'For nothing is set down here but what has been proved by personal experience either of myself or of others, and I, John of Gaddesden, have compiled the whole in the seventh year of my lecture'.

There is little doubt that *Rosa Medicine* was respected in the author's day, and by his immediate successors. As a boy John of Gaddesden had probably gained some of his early knowledge from the monks at Ashridge, near Little Gaddesden, Hertfordshire. (His father, another John of Gaddesden had been a signatory to the original monastic charter.) The poet Chaucer knew him and mentioned him in the Prologue to *The Canterbury Tales* and probably took him as a model for the Doctor of Physick. We get a glimpse of practical medicine in the story that John of Gaddesden attended one of Edward I's sons suffering from smallpox, when he wrapped him in a scarlet cloth in a bed with scarlet hangings. As a treatment for toothache he combined religion with medicine and recommended the words '*Rex Pay in Christo Filio*' be 'written' on the jaw, 'and when the Sunday Gospel is read, let the man sign his tooth and his head with the sign of the Cross and say a paternoster and an ave for the souls of the father and mother of St Philip without stopping'. This, he claimed, would keep pain away in the future and cure his teeth in the present. Some of these early ideas seem to be universally crazy, but herbs were used as well.

Four printed versions were made of *Rosa Medicine*, the earliest in Pavia, Italy, in 1492, and later in Venice 1502 and 1517, and Augsberg 1595. The latter edition updated the arrangement of some of the subject matter and corrected some of the Latin – in other words 'modernized' it more than two and a half centuries later. Even the tragedy of the Plague which ravaged Europe in the mid-fourteenth century seems not to have alerted anyone to investigate disease afresh.

Much was written suggesting ways to combat the Plague, many of them remedies in rhyme form more easily committed to memory. Healing was in the hands of the Almighty and his innumerable saints. Mental and neurological disorders were regarded as they had been since Anglo-Saxon times, as the manifestation of being possessed by a devil.

Opposite:
The mille fleurs *background of many Medieval tapestries confirms the familiarity of many plants, while at the same time adds a highly decorative effect.*

PATRON SAINTS

For medieval Catholics all over Europe each disease had its patron saint, in the way that each had had its Roman god in the Classical world. Tenuously linked was the astrological belief that each planet 'controlled' certain plants and organs of the body; the planets themselves derived their names from the gods. Illness itself was deemed to represent vengeance for past misdemeanours. Therefore sufferers made pilgrimages to the appropriate saints' shrines. Pilgrimages were made also to the location of holy relics as public penance, and to natural springs of water symbolic of the fount of life and known as holy wells. In such a climate of superstition, magic and folk lore, the herbs played a vital and supposedly healing role.

Plants themselves inspired their allocation to a saints' (or planet's) control, possibly suggested by their time of flowering. Garlands, used to adorn statues, had to be of flowers freshly gathered on the appropriate saint's day in the church calendar. Thus among the herbs we find the Christmas rose dedicated to St Agnes, the leek to St David, the shamrock to St Patrick (still recalled in modern ceremonies), the herb Robert to St Robert, St John's wort to St John, costmary to St Mary Magdalen, chamomile to St Anne, wormwood to St Luke, and nigella to St Catherine. Samphire derives its name as a corruption of *Herbe de St Pierre*, St Peter the fisherman being the patron saint of fishermen; the herb grows where it overlooks the sea out of reach of the waves.

MAGIC

Magic is defined as the practice of causing change through the use of powers unidentifiable by science. Much herb lore lies in the realm of magic, which by its very nature is nebulous and vague, and is certainly not meant to be clarified. Originally it was believed that herbal knowledge was revealed to a chosen few by the gods, handed on to Adam by God, or taught to man by angels or Christian saints.

Traditionally herb lore has been handed down from one generation to another by practice and by word of mouth. Written lore has suffered much distortion by inaccurate copying, vague translation, unfamiliarity with the subject and perhaps most forcibly by would-be scholars who have appended their own ideas. Many plants are used the world over in the same way; others vary according to tradition and legend, but these are usually based on faith in the power of the particular plant. Beyond that the attendant magic becomes all powerful, and superstitions, ideas and beliefs about herbs become involved in colours, stars, the moon, the zodiac, saints, and rituals, or the plants are associated with witchcraft and demonology. When herbs were being gathered, certain phases of the moon were to be observed, or perhaps the time of night or day; no iron must touch a herb because it would magnetize the power into itself, withdrawing the virtue of the plant. Added to all this spookery was the secret magic of the Medieval Church. Such attendant mysticism has lent a romance to herbs over the years. The imagination is inhibited and cannot roam. When dragons and sea serpents and mythical beasts 'existed', the imagination was fired, and that in itself was a necessity for magic. Today a rational explanation is forthcoming for the efficacy of a given healing herb simply because the chemical composition of the essential oil is understood.

The magician presides over his spell table, or altar, outdoors, and indulges in symbolic ritual to cast a spell. Plants and plant material played a vital role in such rites.

The bygone world created their own magical systems and attendant tools of the trade; the candle, the censer, the non-metal bowl for brewing potions, a time piece and the all powerful incantation. A spell table or altar of some sort, indoors or out, lent (and still does lend) a religious association, albeit little more than faith and expectancy. Spells related perhaps to a person, a need, or to the four elements, had (maybe still have!) particular uses in magic. Earth concerned prosperity, fertility, healing, fulfilment of purpose; Air related to the spiritual and mental powers and to the psychic; Fire represented courage, robust health, strength and lust; while Water was concerned with love, friendship, sleep and fidelity. Then there were masculine and feminine herbs, and their ruling planet according to astrological botany had to be observed, their sympathies and antipathies, their power to produce some disposition of the mind or change in moral intent. All manner of contrived cunning credited plants with supernatural powers, invariably stemming from ancient man-made reasons. Today, the four-leaved clover is still associated with good luck because in the magical world it had the power to drive out witches.

Herbs associated with magical intentions

FIDELITY: *cumin, elder, liquorice, periwinkle*

HAPPINESS: *catnep, lavender, marjoram, purslane, saffron, St John's wort*

LONGEVITY: *lavender, sage, tansy*

WEALTH: *basil, chamomile, comfrey, cowslip, dill, elder, marjoram, mint, vervain*

PROTECTION: *agrimony, angelica, anise, basil, bay, burdock, comfrey, elecampane, fennel, foxglove, herb bennet, horehound, hyssop, marigold, mugwort, nettle, orris, plantain, rosemary, sage, violet, wormwood*

LOVE: *basil, catnep, chamomile, coltsfoot, coriander, dill, elecampane, eryngo, lavender, lemon balm, lovage, marjoram, meadowsweet, peppermint, periwinkle, primrose, rose, rosemary, southernwood, thyme, valerian, violet, yarrow*

During this period the 'voodoo doll' emerged from the mists of time. Records of its involvement apparently exist from as far back as 4000 BC. A doll, or 'pupette' as it is sometimes known, purports to be a representation of the person for whom, or upon whom the magic is to be wrought. Fashioned out of roots, tubers, bark and adorned with seeds, fruits or leaves, the image then provided a receptacle for the magic. As late as the nineteenth century, itinerant herb men offered 'ready-made' such figures for sale.

Such magical powers were vested in particular in the mandrake (*Mandragora officinarum*), the long dark root of which was shaped like man. Its powers over sleep and death, with intermediate madness made it sacred to the moon goddess Selene, who happened also to be the goddess of witchcraft. Thus in Medieval England the mandrake automatically became *the* witching plant. Added to a witch's cauldron with henbane and various animal products its alkaloids caused hallucinations, convincing the witch herself that she was soaring through the sky. The root is recorded as being used in surgical anaesthetics in Persia 3000 years ago, and mandrake wine or mandrake ale was a conventional treatment, sometimes being administered for common insomnia. The true mandrake was sometimes difficult to find, so the root of bryony (*Bryonia dioica*) or devil's turnip was substituted and pupettes created in the form of a man. Mystery, sorcery and fear surrounded the mandrake, and it is still endowed with a magic (mis)understanding. Earlier in the *Leech Book of Bald*, the plant was reported to shine at night 'altogether like a lamp' which in more factual terms is explained because glow worms, attracted by the fragrance, settle among the large rosette of leaves!

Fairies

When the imagination ranged into the realms of wishing, perhaps for the impossible, let alone the improbable, the fairies had to be invoked. Wood sorrel and thyme and foxgloves were of particular value. Fairy folk it is said, clothed themselves in foxgloves. The name foxglove derives from folks' glove — the fairies being known as little folk — their hair was dodder, their carriages hazel nuts and their fairy steeds ragwort seed.

TO ENABLE ONE TO SEE THE FAIRIES

A pint of sallet oyle and put it into a vial glasse: and first wash it with rose-water and marigolde water; the flowers be gathered towards the east. Wash it until the oyle becomes white, then put it into the glasse and then put thereto the budds of hollyhocke, the flowers of marygolde, the flowers or toppes of wild thyme, the budd of young hazel and the thyme must be gathered near the side of a hill where the fairies used to be; and take the grasse of a fairy throne, then all these put into the oyle in the glasse and sette it to dissolve three days in the sun, and keep it for thy use.

Connections between plants and fairies are not merely romantic figments trailing with us from childhood, but gossamer threads of plant folklore, and because all plants were herbs in the dark past, folk lore, or fairy lore is a tangle of beliefs that have never developed in keeping with contemporary thinking but have remained a fantasy of practices and legends. Every wild plant was endowed with some power; many are no longer recorded and even more are no longer considered to be useful herbs.

COLOURFUL MIRACLES

A further remarkable talent that plants displayed was that they provided a range of colours which would dye cloth. The Romans had known that plants produced different colours under different conditions and that some fixative or mordant was needed. To the Medieval world only a limited and relatively muted range of colour was available. Woad (*Isatis tinctoria*) associated with the Ancient Britons and Saxons produced a blue dye after a tedious process of fermenting and combining with lime water, a colour commemorated as saxe-blue. Weld (*Reseda luteola*) produced yellow or according to the mordant, green or blue, which, when mixed with woad, produced green, probably the Lincoln green of Robin Hood; this plant was far easier to use, the whole plant being boiled in water after collecting it from pastures or waste land. Dyer's rocket was its vernacular name, and remains so today. Dyer's broom or dyer's greenweed (*Genistra tinctoria*) was sometimes taken in from the wild and cultivated in parts of Kent and around Kendal in Cumbria, to provide a green dye. Saffron was extensively cultivated primarily to colour food a rich yellow. It produced a good dye for cloth also, but 60 000 yellow stigmas were required for 0.45 kg (1 lb) and it has been estimated that an acre of land upheld sufficient for 10.8 kg (24 lb) of dried stigmas. Walnut husks and the roots of the water lily provided various browns.

Some lichens gave a range of browns, dull reds, orange and yellows, and in the unpolluted woodlands they were far more plentifully available than in the present day. Corklit or cudbear, the precursor of cochineal, was important: this, when soaked in stale urine with chalk added, gave a bright red for soldiers' coats for many years. (There are records of the collection of 13 650 l (3000 gal) a day of urine in Glasgow for the dyers.) Lichens also were the chief source of colouring from medieval times onward, in the production of tartans and the warm colours of Harris tweed. Crottle or crotal, sometimes called staneraw, provided an orange brown, and black crottle (*kenderig* in Wales) a reddish brown. The root of lady's bedstraw (*Galium verum*) gave a red dye, bracken (*Pteridium aquilinum*) a brown one and gipsywort (*Lycopus europaeus*) got its name from the use as a primitive 'sun tan' by early gipsies who tinted their skin brown.

Madder (*Rubia tinctoria*) was difficult to cultivate in Britain, and was imported in quantity from the Low Countries (Netherlands) and Flanders (France) for the expanding woollen trade. Good reds and browns were obtainable from it, and it was sometimes employed as hair colour, after peeling the root, heating and pulverizing. The juice of the stem curdled milk to form a curd cheese. Soon the explorers were bringing back rich dye materials such as safflower (*Carthamnus tinctoria*) and fustic (*Chloraphora tinctoria*), and from the fifteenth century onwards the dyer's trade began to assume semi-industrial levels. Other imported dyes of the period included orchil (violet), copperas (green), annatto (near-red), barwood (red) and camwood (red).

HERB GATHERERS

Much material for both dyeing and household remedy, was, as we have seen, gathered from the countryside, and during the Middle Ages the apothecaries were regarded as little more than drug pedlars or remedy merchants. They were to be found at fairs and markets offering love philtres, poisons and medicinal herbs. Scant records remain of the succession of ordinary people skilled in the use of herbs but midwives and 'old' women and 'green' men who moved about localities were depended upon for supplies. Green men themselves were 'endowed' with fantastic ritual ability ranging over both crops and human beings and became supremely important fourteenth- and fifteenth-century symbols. Bench ends and corbels in county churches of the period sometimes depict a green man with stylized foliage bursting from his ears, head or mouth and here is unquestioned evidence of the popular importance of such rural characters. That the Church would tolerate such pagan symbolism inside its buildings only confirms the unflinching grip of the superstition. Pedlars of herbs were known as green men for another four or five hundred years, although as the centuries passed they became little more than charlatans or herb vendors. Their role in the community is commemorated by the Green Man inn sign today.

The collection of herbs from their natural habitat persisted through the centuries, so that a wealth of regional remedies often relating to local plants remain as part of British folk medicine. Anglo-Saxon and Medieval medicine was a mish-mash of paganism, Christianity and Latin lore.

The Medieval health book Tacuinum sanitatis *included instructions in the employment of herbs.*

Dill: 'It is good for cold and damp temperaments, for old people, in Winter and in cold regions'.

Marjoram: 'It is good for a cold and humid stomach'.

Herbs from afar

Devoid of attendant ritual and superstition were some of the imported materials, spices in particular, that came into the country for medicines and food, even in Anglo-Saxon times. As the centuries passed the spice trade flourished and commodities were handled by the pepperers and spicers of London — later to become the grocers and apothecaries. The fourteenth century brought a demand for a certain refinement in medicaments and this was met by the true apothecaries rather than the grocery trade. The first apothecary's shop in London opened in 1345. Both the pepperers and the spice-apothecaries agitated to establish standards for the drugs sold, in their own interest to overcome fraudulent practices. Every age has had its opportunists and there were frequent claims that herbs and spices had been adulterated by inferior and less expensive products. In 1393 the Company of Grocers appointed members to inspect the crude drugs for both purity and weight, and assigned them as Garblers.

Great Italian galleons navigated the river Thames bringing drugs and spices from the (Middle) East until the fifteenth century, when imports were diverted to Southampton, a port then expanding with the wool trade. These imports were distributed at Medieval fairs, for example the Lenten fair at Nottingham, St Bartolph's at Boston, St Giles' at Winchester, and by the merchants and pedlars. In Oxford, as early as the thirteenth century a district around St Mary's was called Apothecaria. Later herbs and drugs were sold wholesale by the London companies and provincial distribution centres were established such as those at York, Chester, Bristol and Norwich.

Some imported dried plant material may seem surprising, but serves to reflect the demand and size of the market. Caraway and coriander seed came measured in hundred-weights; hellebore, saffron, sea holly, senna, wormseed, acorns, alkanet, angelica, licorice, bugle, gentian and even juniper berries all appear in bulk in various lists of imports.

THE FEATE OF GARDENING

Meanwhile the craft of cultivating plants, almost all of them herbs, roots and fruit, was developing. A treatise written in verse by Mayster Jan (John) Gardener c. 1400–1440 is generally considered to be a copy made of some earlier work, and John Gardener is the *nom de plume* of the copyist. What qualifies it as a salient waymark in the history of gardening is the practical down-to-earth approach to the craft of gardening

A physic garden in which apothecaries confer and instruct, while herbs are gathered and prepared as medicines. Top left: the fictitious patient who is to benefit.

unencumbered by personal asides on the plants from the author. Superstition is not recorded, practical gardening is, but it is not for the instructive value that it claims importance here but for the list of plants — all of which are herbs in the widest sense. Several afforded delight such as daffodil, honeysuckle and water lily and reveal that no longer was the monopoly on cultivated plants held by the monasteries and aristocrats, but that they were grown also by country squires, merchants, yeomen and farmers. John Gardener listed almost a hundred plants, many of them native; others such as lavender, Madonna lily, primrose and scabious are decorative plants today and the majority of the remaining plants were medicinal herbs, or herbs used for their aroma or flavour. Some, such as herb Robert, hawkweed, plantain and adder's tongue, are today sequestering back in the countryside whence they came; only the common daisy has stayed about organized gardens, where in spite of its demure charm it is treated as a weed.

A garden, illustrated in 1500, where herbs are being gathered and distilled. Note the pond and drinking fountain and the simply constructed wattle fence.

THE FROMOND LIST

Nearly a century later, a far fuller list of plants including a wide range of herbs was more concerned with the domestic *purpose* for which they were cultivated. It represents, as far as we know, the earliest attempt in England to categorize garden plants (c. 1500) and comes from the beginning of a cookery book of recipies belonging to Thomas Fromond of Carshalton, Surrey. He arranged the names of 138 plants as 'Herbys necessary for a gardyn by letter'; in other words alphabetically. He then enumerated them as 'Herbes for the copp [cup], Herbes for a Salade, Herbez to Stylle, Herbes fo[r] Savour and beaute and Rotys [roots] for a gardyn'. They are listed below.

A. Alysaundre, Avence, Astralogia rotunda, Astralogia longa, Alleluia, Arcachaff, Artemesie mogwede, Annes, Archangel

B. Borage, Betes, Betyeyn, Basilican, Bugle, Burnett

C. Cabage, Chervell, Carewey, Cyves, Columbyn, Clarey, Colyaundr', Colewort, Cartabus, Cressez, Cressez of Bolyeyn, Calamyntes, Camamyll, Ceterwort

D. Daysez, Dyteyn, Daundelyon, Dragaunce, Dylle

E. Elena campana, Eufras, Egremoyn

F. Fenell, Foothistell, Fenecreke

G. Gromell, Goldez, Byllofr', Germaundr'

H. Hertez tonge, Horehound, Henbane

I. Isope, Ierlin, Iryngez, herbe Ive

K. Kykombre, yt. bereth apples

L. Longdebeff, Lekez, Letuse, Loveache, Lympons, Lylle, Longwortz

M. Mercury, Malowes, Mytes, Mageron, Mageron gentyle, Mandrake, Mylone

N. Nept, Nettell rede, Nardus capiscola

O. Orage, Oculus Christi, Oynons

P. Persely, Pelytore, Pelytore of Spayn, Puliall royall, Pyper white, Pacyence, Popy whit', Prymerose, Purselane, Philipendula

Q. Qvyncez

R. Rapes, Radyched, Rampsons, Rapouncez, Rokettes, Rewe

S. Sauge, Saverey, Spynache, Sede-wale, Scalaceli, Smalache, Sauce alone, Selbestryue, Syves, Sorell, Sowthistell, Sothernwode, Skabiose, Selian, Stycadose, Stanmarch

T. Tyme, Tansey

V. Vyolettes, Wermode, Wormesdede, Verveyn

Herbes for Potage

The list that Mr Fromard compiled reveals substantial proof of the way in which herbs were used. We see that mercury, rape, lettuce, spinach, orach and such leaf plants were used in stews, and mallow, avens, columbine, daisy, catmint and betony were included.

For flavouring drinks alecost, sage, hyssop, rosemary, pinks, marigolds (with the lovely name of goldez or goldies), clary, rue and marjoram were brought to use. The three main staples of diet in England at that time were bread, pottage and ale. Pottage included flesh, oatmeal and chopped vegetables and, apparently, flowers. The cereals were ground at home with a hand quern or in a mortar which resulted in a bran-like stew thickener into which eggs were sometimes mixed, or saffron to render the colour more appetizing.

Fromond's complete list of *Herbes for Potage* included: borage, langdebefe (viper's bugloss), vyolette, malowes, mercury, caundelyon, avence (avens), mynt, sauge, percely, goldes (marigold), mageron, fenell, caroway, rednettyll, oculus curisti (clary), daysys, chervell, lekez, betayn (betony), columbyn, alla (woodsorrel?), astrologia rotunda (round birthwort), astrologia longa (long birthwort), basillican (basil), dyll, deteyn (dittany), egrymon, hertstory, radiche, white pyper, cobagez, sedewale (setwall) spynache, coliaunar, roothistyll (sowthistle), orage, cartabus (cardoon?), lympons (lupins), Nepte, clarey, pacience.*

Herbs used variously

Apparently sauces were concocted to include hart's-tongue, sorrel, two kinds of pellitory, dittany, violet, parsley and mint. To flavour beverages, Fromond lists costmary, sage, hyssop, rosemary, gillyflower, clarey, marjoram and rue. In a salad he would have Alexander's (buds) violet flowers, parsley, mints, chives, watercress, purslane, calamint, rose buds, daisies, campion, dandelion, rocket, nettle, borage flowers, sprigs of black fennel (Fromond described it as red fennel which does better

Rose: 'Good for inflamed brains;
Danger: in some persons they cause headaches'.

Rue: 'It sharpens the eyesight and dissipates flatulence'.

---

* The identification of plants is acknowledged from *Early Gardening Catalogues*, by John H. Harvey (1973).

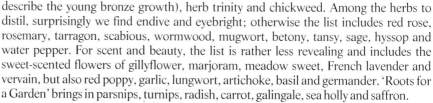

describe the young bronze growth), herb trinity and chickweed. Among the herbs to distil, surprisingly we find endive and eyebright; otherwise the list includes red rose, rosemary, tarragon, scabious, wormwood, mugwort, betony, tansy, sage, hyssop and water pepper. For scent and beauty, the list is rather less revealing and includes the sweet-scented flowers of gillyflower, marjoram, meadow sweet, French lavender and vervain, but also red poppy, garlic, lungwort, artichoke, basil and germander. 'Roots for a Garden' brings in parsnips, turnips, radish, carrot, galingale, sea holly and saffron.

Following these practical lists of economic plants, Fromond gives us a glimpse of decorative gardening of his times and regales a number of plants 'for an Herber'. A herber was an arbour or small shaded or secluded garden and in it he recommends vines, roses, lilies, dewberries (*Rubus* sp.), almonds, sweet bay, gourds, date tree (all exotics were of interest!), peach trees, pineapple (not the plant of that name today), peonies, campions, columbine and hellebore. He adds one or two more vernacular names that do not suggest familar plants today, such as cartabus and selyan.

CHAUCER'S FLOWERS

The lists of Master John Gardener and of Fromond give a fairly clear idea of the herbs grown in ordinary fourteenth- and fifteenth-century gardens, and known to the common people. Chaucer's works are scattered with many references to common flowers he knew well, as if his whole mind were a flowery mead.

> *Ful gay wis al the ground and queynt*
> *And powdred as men had it peynt,*
> *With many a fresh and sundry flour*
> *That casten up a ful good savour.*

Romant of the Rose

STREWING

It is abundantly obvious that plants provided every need, even in a way which today seems limited. When indoor floors were of stone or earth, it was customary to spread a layer of gathered plant material over them. Strewing in this way was a common practice in Britain and other northern European countries from early times until the late eighteenth century. Even in the nineteenth century it was continued in such places as closets and musky church pews. The purpose in Medieval halls, churches and humble dwellings was to render stone or earth floors warmer in winter, and to deter vermin, insects and frogs. Rushes were used in aristocratic places (there are records of sweet rushes being imported from the Netherlands) and aromatic plants were mixed among them; these obviously are the northern European native plants that grew about the villages and were to hand. Flea repellent or antiseptic and sweet-smelling herbs were the favourites, like juniper, wormwood, fleabane, fennel, costmary, mints, woodruff, marjoram, sweet flag, meadowsweet, rue and tansy. Later lavender, santolina and rosemary were included in the resilient absorbent floor covering. Pennyroyal gained its Latin suffix of *pulegium* because it was effective in banishing fleas from habitations. It is reputed that Thomas à Beckett ordered the hall at Canterbury to be strewn afresh each day in spring with fresh sweet rushes 'that such knights as the benches could not contain might sit on the floor without dirtying their clothes'. Unfortunately scented rushes attracted fleas, so it was customary to burn fleabane when the rushes were removed and a fresh supply brought in.

One of the country names for meadowsweet is bridewort because this was the favourite plant for strewing at wedding festivals. Michael Drayton writing of his Warwickshire countryside says

> *Among these strewing kinds some other wild that grow*
> *As burnet all abroad and meadowwort they throw.*

HOUSEHOLD CRAFTS

Not only was woman's work confined to planting, gathering and cooking with herbs and harbouring household remedies, but to providing numerous domestic appliances. Among these were scourers for pots and cooking utensils, formed from a fistful of horsetails (*Equisetum* sp.) or sieves made from a goodly layer of goosegrass (*Galium aparine*). Small bunches of birch twigs served as egg whisks and food mixers, while stouter twigs bound together served as brooms. The soapy content of soapwort or bouncing Bet was well known to the housewife. When agitated in water a cleansing foam is produced, recorded in the rural name for the plant of crowsope or foam dock. Its other name of fuller's grass confirms its use for washing fleeces, and probably mashed horsechestnuts were employed in the same way.

Chandling was another home craft, where rushes were dipped in fat to burn to provide light. The native soft rush (*Juncus effusus*) which grew abundantly in the ill-drained countryside was gathered, soaked for a while, then dried out of doors. The outer skin was stripped from the pith which was then slipped into whatever fat was to hand – bacon fat, mutton fat, dripping, lard — and allowed to drain. Simple traditional holders held the 'candle' which when lit emitted a bright concentrated light and a smell of roasting meat. The refinement of incorporating aromatic herbs to the tallow seems to have been a much later development.

When we look at the erect resinous spikes of the mullein, it is not surprising that it was used in the same way. It was commonly burnt in churches and used as a torchlight in processions, gaining it the country names of high taper, torches and Aaron's rod.

THE DECLINE OF MAGIC

Magic and folklore trail on forming a thread of unreason through the centuries. Amid the disorder in England, and Europe in general, up to the millenium, herbs played a vital, almost enveloping role in the short brutish lives of the people. It is impossible to separate herbal practice or folk lore from magic, from paganism and superstition and from the power of the Medieval church. Ritualistic thinking hampered any rational advance in medicine. A plant, a herb no less, was empowered to celebrate festivals, bury the dead, treat warts, dog bites, bring rain, cause love to flourish or portend death. By the turn of the sixteenth century although some order glimmered ahead, there was still a profound dependence upon herbs. Few rich and stable legacies were to remain around plants as the basis of trade — the making of liqueurs, the value of plant narcotics — although at that time their power was to transport the experience to realms where the gods could be understood.

II

GARDENS OF DELIGHT
(1500–1650)

But absolutely free
His happy time he spends the works of God to see,
In those so sundry herbs which there in plenty grow
Whose sundry strange effects he only seeks to know;
And in a little maund, being made of osiers small
Which serveth him to do full many a thing withal,
He very choicely sorts his simples, got abroad;
Here he finds on an oak rheum-purging Polypode;
And in some open place that to the sun doth lie,
He Fumitory gets, and Euyebright for the eye
The Yarrow wherewithal he stays the wound made gore,
The healing Tutsan then, and Plantaine for a sore;
And hard by them again the holy Vervain finds
Which he about his head that hath the megrim binds;
The wonder-working Dill he gets not far from these,
Which curious women use in many a nice disease;
For them that are with newts, or snakes or adders stung
He seeketh out a herb that is called Adder's tongue;
As Nature it ordain'd its own like hurt to cure
And sportive did herself to niceties inure.
Valerian he then crops and purposely doth stamp
To apply unto the place that's haled with the cramp;
The chickweed cures the heat that in the face doth rise,
For physic some again he inwardly applies,
For comforting the spleen and liver, gets for juice
Pale Horehound, which he holds of most especial use.
And for the labouring wretch that's troubled with a cough
Or stopping of the breath by phlegm that's hard and tough
Campana here he crops approved wondrous good;
Or Comfrey into him that's bruised, spitting blood;
And for the falling ill by Five-leafe doth restore,
And melancholy cures by sovereign Hellebore.
Of these most helpful herbs yet tell me but a vew
To those unnumbered sorts of simples here that grew,
What justly to set down even Dodon short doth fall
Nor skilful Gerarde yet shall ever find them all.

Michael Drayton, Polyalbion (1622)

TUDOR GARDENING

Life in England gradually became more settled as the sixteenth century opened with attendant changes in social life. No longer was it essential to protect property by moat or stout wall, so delightfully elaborate houses of timber or stonework with sparkling glass windows were erected by the newly rising families. They displayed their wealth by making fantastic and decorative gardens, in keeping with the taste of the age. Equally, the country squire and merchant built more modest houses probably surrounded by water, and beyond that a garden or orchard area would be set aside. In some instances the garden was within a courtyard of the building where formality seemed appropriate. It was this formality that was the germination of English garden design. Previously, for centuries, plants had been cultivated in rows (indeed they were to continue to be grown in this way for centuries to come) but it was the Tudor gardeners who first expressed their delight in plants and had fun with them. The beds would be arranged in some symmetrical way, associating the plot more closely with the building, and plants would be used far more decoratively than ever before.

Knots

The knotted bed or knot garden had its inception in this period and became intricate and quite sophisticated in form. Over the following 150 years, the knot would be based upon a simple geometric design that could be contained in a square, rectangle or circle. Contemporary gardening books display a variety of suggested patterns of 'proper knots', although it seems doubtful that some could ever have been transferred successfully to the ground. Blake wrote in rhyme when designing his knots in *The Complete Gardener's Practice*.

> *Cross Diamonds in the paper I doe frame*
> *And in the ground I can draw the same.*
> *Four severall (separate) quarters fit for to be drawne*
> *With herbe or box for to set Flowers there in.*

Patterns were outlined in one kind of plant; box, lavender, germander, rosemary, lavender cotton are each suggested, but by the early seventeenth century, Parkinson told us that box was by far the most successful and that the attraction of this evergreen pattern was that it offered year-round interest. Even as the winter snows thawed, the pattern of the knot began to reappear, traced by the plants melting the snow above them first.

Expressly suited to a level site, such knotted presentations could be made comparatively quickly in preparation for an event. We read of knots being made below the Queen's casement, towards the end of the sixteenth century, when the Court was relocating. Such formal patterns were viewed to perfection from above.

The effect was achieved by close planting and later close clipping whichever plant was to outline the pattern, to give the effect of ribbons intertwined. The spaces between were filled either by flowers in season, or by coloured earth and shale, or by pebbles or shells to adorn the pattern. Ideally an engagingly painted patchwork of flowers emerged, although in practice planting was sparse, formed of cowslips, violets, heartsease, marigolds, cornflowers, columbines, double daisies, 'gilded marjoram', pot marjoram, pinks, periwinkle, herba-grace (rue), sage and auriculas. We cannot help wondering how seasonal such foibles became, or just how universally popular they were, for maybe there were others besides Bacon who disapproved: 'They be but toys' he wrote 'you may see as good sights many times in tarts'. Undoubtedly these 'toys' still capture our attention as if they were the only novelty conjured up by the Elizabethan gardeners. What busy exciting days those were, with orchards and parks and *al fresco* amusements laid on in arbours and herbers. What wondrous outlandish plants were being introduced, curious and intriguing.

Low rails turned in elm and painted sometimes surrounded the knots. Not only would these curb romping children and dogs, but served to preserve plants from being brushed by gowns and cloaks. Further it suggests that for the first time in England a garden design was contained and free access within the design was to be discouraged.

From Cats Emblems, *1622, a garden showing the gateway to an 'Elizabethan Herb Garden'. Note the crown imperial (*Fritillaria imperialis*) *and tulips introduced half a century earlier. Musing upon the significance of the winged boy, adds a sense of ancient mystery.*

Elsewhere plants were grown in borders 'thin and sparingly, lest they deceive the trees' (rob them of nourishment), although today we know that it is the trees that are the gross drinkers! Open beds, of the Medieval style persisted, often with the new name of 'open knots' and sometimes edged with stags' horns or animal skulls or other whimsical objects.

Newcomers

Once a new decorative plant was acquired it was almost always grown in a pot, so that it could be transported and admired and it is not improbable that once the plant had been propagated successfully, subsequent generations were planted in the open beds. Many of the newcomers were blatantly unsuited to cultivation in knot beds, and certainly had no economic value. These plants had no folk lore, no harvest time, no familiar name but were intriguing botanical curios. The arrival, dispersal and increasing popularity of them led to enlightened botanical knowledge on the one hand and a wider acceptance of decorative flower gardens on the other: botany and horticulture.

Some herbs also were newly introduced about the same period, and were added to the apothecaries' palette quite quickly because they arrived as economic plants and knowledge of their uses preceded them. Calamintha came from Italy in the 1590s, *Gentiana lutea* (gentian bitters) from the European Alps came at the same time, lemon balm from Southern Europe in 1573, nasturtium (*Tropaeolum majus*) from South America in 1597 (which the Tudor gardeners trained as climbers on trellises and arbours in the way that they grew runner beans for their pied red flowers), valerian from the Middle East in 1597, thyme (*Thymus vulgaris*) from Southern Europe in 1548 and dyer's madder from Europe in 1596.

Harrison who wrote *A Description of England* between 1577 and 1587 says of gardens that the exotic plants were grown by 'noblemen, gentlemen and merchants', but that in gardens 'annexed to our houses, how wonderfully is their beauty increased, not only with flowers, but also with rare and medicinal herbs . . . so that in comparison of this present, the ancient gardens were but dunghills'. In the same work, writing about the number of herbs newly introduced, he argues the fallibility of 'foreign herbs' introduced from the Caucasus and Greece on the grounds that the populace there 'are of another constitution than ours are here at home'.

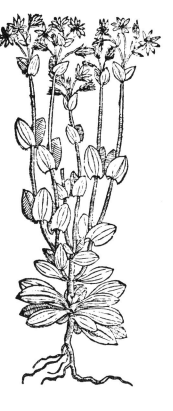

GARDENS OF DELIGHT

Gardeners and observers on all sides were aware of the way in which 'exoticks' enriched their gardens and their gardening knowledge and yet clearly the herbs were the most important product of the garden. The sixteenth century was the hey-day of herbs, medicinal, culinary and aromatic, and it is therefore not surprising that for historical reference to herb gardens today we go back to Elizabethan ideas.

The inventive gardeners erected a range of arbours and arcades, walks and intricate railings, posts and poles all designed to support flowery twining plants to decorate and make sweet smelling shady places for strolling and sitting in — such a delight to get out from their fetid houses!

Arcades could be formed temporarily if necessary for some *al fresco* event, of wood when branches were entwined to provide shade. Such shaded walks made of so-called 'carpenter's work' as more permanent structures formed the perimeter of a garden where perhaps the enclosed area would be set with a knot or series of knots. Alternatively, such arcades or galleries were punctuated by arbours or 'roosting places' provided with a bank or bench for dallying where in the grander gardens music could be made, games played, or sewing done.

In the way that the Anglo-Saxons had believed in imaginary 'little folk', the sixteenth-century fancies flew to fabulous animals; some, like the dragon, unicorn and griffon were relics of the Medieval mind; other beasts and birds were carved in wood or stone, and set atop painted posts. In Hampton Court garden the King had 38 beasts to adorn his garden and Queen Elizabeth enjoyed elaborately decorated beasts in her garden at Whitehall. 'Birds, beasts and pyramids do grow speedily' said Sir Hugh Platt some time later (1655) and tells us how a hollow wooden frame can be constructed or a clay model formed and adorned with sprigs of hyssop, thyme and rosemary.

Smaller gardens

In the more modest gardens of manor houses or town gardens belonging to merchants, the fantasy would be contained to a knot or to some form of sundial perhaps of painted wood, with a suitable inscription confirming the fleeting course of time. Today we have a parallel in that suburban gardens are not described; thus, the tiny garths of cottages and the buildings that clustered about the churches or farms go unrecorded. In such enclosures without much doubt, bee hives, carts and poultry would be littered among the apple tree, gooseberry bush and kale. Maybe some caring housewife had collected primroses, cowslips, woundwort, yarrow and mints from the countryside and marigolds, clove pinks, wallflowers or a rose were possibly also included in the plot.

Nosegay gardens

An array of scented and melliferous plants would be grown in one part of the garden – a gardening habit that has persisted — and designated the nosegay garden. Gervase Markham wrote in 1616, copied from earlier writing: 'These sweet herbes and flowers for nosegaies shall be set in order upon beds and quarters of such like length and breadth, as those of a kitchen garden, and some of them on seats'. Plants beloved for their fragrance of flower or leaf were assembled there to give added pleasure to garden

A learning book, Visible World *(1664) by J A Comenius proclaims that pot herbs grow in gardens.*

Pot-herbs grow in
Gardens,
as, Lettice, 1.
Colewort, 2.
Onions, 3.

In hortis nafcuntur
Olera,
ut, *Lactuca*, 1.
Braffica, 2.
Cepa, 3.

C 3   Gar

dalliance. Lavender, rosemary, pinks, catnep, jasmine, roses, mints, lilies, artemisias, sweet William, cowslips, dame's violet, violets, lily-of-the-valley or conval lily as it was called, and a collection of gillyflowers were all there. Wallflowers too, or wall gillyflowers as they were known (their very name *Cheiranthus* means 'hand flower'), were a prime choice for nosegays. Nasturtiums were classed as scented and were trained to festoon posts and arbours and were recommended for tussie-mussies, or hand posies of scented flowers offered to guests. Honeysuckles (or to give them their older name, woodbine) and eglantine (*Rosa rubiginosa*) twisted over trellis along with the carnival flowers of runner bean, grown then for their flowers rather than their juicy pods. Later in the period, great flowering shrubs, almost unknown in England gardens previously, were added to the nosegay garden; lilac (*Syringa vulgaris*) and mock orange (*Philadelphus coronaria*) both from Turkey, found their way into the hearts of the Stuarts.

TUSSIE-MUSSIES

John Parksinson is often credited with first recording his delightful vernacular name for scented nosegays, but it had been used as tuttie, tuttymose or tutty for at least four centuries, appearing as tuzzie muzzie in a 1033 manuscript. A lexicon of 1440 gives 'Tyte Tust or Tusmore of Flowrys or other herbys' and Thomas Campion wrote:

Joan can call by name her cows,
And deck her windows with green bows.
She can wreathes and tuttyes make
And trim with plums a bridal cake.

Several 'olfactorum' references confirm that nosegays were carried about the person, sometimes dangling from the girdle.

A Billet Douce

The giving of a small nosegay to an arriving or departing guest became a popular custom and there is some evidence of it being practised in earlier times. Now the gift itself could convey a message; earlier symbolism was carried into everyday life and treated far more lightheartedly by the fun-loving Elizabethans. Where the meaning of a flower was understood by both donor and recipient, nosegays or tussie-mussies could be contrived to convey a loving message or a single sentiment. William Hunnis an Elizabethan lyricist recorded the key to this delightful language:

Lavender is for lovers true
Which evermore be fain,
Desiring always for to have
Some pleasure for their pain:
And when that they obtained have
The love that they require,
Then have they all their perfect joy,
And quenched is the fire.

Rosemary is for remembrance
Between us day and night;
Wishing that I might always have
You present in my sight.
And when I cannot have
As I have said before,
Then Cupid with his deadly dart
Doth wound my heart full sore.

Sage is for sustenance,
That should man's life sustain;
For I do still lie languishing
Continually in pain,
And shall do still until I die
Except thou favour' show:
My pain and all my grievous smart
Full well you do it know.

Fennel is for flatterers,
An evil thing it is sure,
But I have always meant truly,
With constant heart most pure;
And will continue in the same
As long as life doth last,
Still hoping for a joyful day
When all our pains be past.

Violet is for faithfulness,
Which in me shall abide;
Hoping likewise that from your heart
You will not let it slide:
And will continue in the same
As you have now begun;
And then for ever to abide;
Then you my heart have won.

Thyme is to try me,
As each be tried must,
Letting you know while life doth last
I will not be unjust;
And if I should, I would to God
To hell my soul should bear,
And eke also that Belzebub
With teeth he should me tear.

Roses is to rule me
With reason as you will,
For to be still obedient
Your mind for to fulfil;
And thereto will not disagree
In nothing that you say,
But will content your mind truly
In all things that I may.

Gillyflowers is for gentleness,
Which in me shall remain,
Hoping that no sedition shall
Depart our hearts in twain.
As soon the sun shall lose his course,
The moon against her kind
Shall have no light, if that I do
Once put you from my mind.

Carnations is for graciousness,
Mark that now by the way,
Have no regard to flatterers,
Nor pass not what they say.
For they will come with lying tales,
Your ears for to fulfil:
In any case do not consent
Nothing unto their will.

Marigolds is for marriage,
That would our minds suffice,
Lest that suspicion of us twain
By any means should rise;
As for my part, I do not care,
Myself I will still use,
That all the women in the world
For you I will refuse.

Pennyroyal is to print your love
So deep within my heart,
That when you look this nosegay on,
My pain you may impart;
And when that you have read the same,
Consider well my woe,
Think ye then how to recompense
Even him that loves you so.

Cowslips is for counsel,
For secrets us between,
That none but you and I alone
Should know the thing we mean:
And if you will thus wisely do,
As I think to be best,
Then have you surely won the field
And set my heart at rest.

I pray you keep this nosegay well,
And set by it some store;
And thus farewell! the gods thee guide
Both now and evermore!
Not as the common sort do use,
To set it in your breast,
That when the smell is gone away,
On ground he takes his rest.

THOMAS TUSSER (1524? – 1580)

When Thomas Tusser retired from life at Court and became a smallholder in the village of Cattiwade, Suffolk, little did he realize that the simple writing would gain him recognition over more than four centuries. He wrote the first vernacular verse in a nursery-rhyme style in 1557 as *Five hundred points of good husbandrie.* The small quarto publication of 13 folios in block letter, set out in 109 quatrains describes work in a rural community and the country calendar form. He dedicated it to his patron, Lord Paget, secretary of State, who had guided his education both at St Paul's School, London, and at Trinity Hall, Cambridge. It seems that although the young Thomas Tusser originated from simple East Anglian yeoman farming stock, he possessed an outstanding singing voice which was to procure for him favoured and continued patronage. Tusser relates his own life story in an uninhibited fashion in the later editions of his book, which following his marriage became extended to include *Five hundred points of good husbandrie united to as many of good housewiferie* (1573) which proved to be a Tudor best seller. Married twice and moving about East Anglia, Tusser appears to have been a drifter, returning to the agricultural community on two occasions when his patrons died. He was described as a man who 'impoverished himself, and never enriched his landlord'.

Nevertheless, it is from Tusser that we have a countryman's description of country life in the mid-sixteenth century, and his detailed lists of herbs commonly cultivated, some of which are not widely known today. He saw no need to describe the gardens, which would be simple plots with plants set in rows or blocks, cheek by jowl with gooseberry bushes, apple or pear trees and often overrun by poultry. Occasionally he defines a tool or mentions a regular gardening practice; otherwise he describes harvesting, weeding, sheep dipping, mole catching, sawing over the saw pit, and attending to horses, bees, thatch and drains, brewing, candle-making, malting, felling and diet. Moreover housewives are instructed to go to the woods and collect strawberry plants (these would be *Fragaria vesca*). From him we know how hops and saffron and flax were managed. For the interest here, we look at what he had to say about herbs which were so much a part of everyday life.

Herbs to growe for physic

Tusser's catalogue of herbs 'to growe in the garden for physick' seems incredibly modest. However he qualifies it by adding 'not rehearsed before', in other words, not appearing in the lists elsewhere. The majority of plants were endowed with several virtues as healing herbs, or as a specific for a common ailment and many, of course, were depended upon to raise the spirits, or treat 'the whole person' in today's parlance.

Herbs, branches and flowers for windows and pots

Most appealing is Tusser's list of flowers for cutting as if it were almost taken for granted that they were accorded special places where they could be seen and enjoyed. There is also the suggestion that the decorative plants were brought in purely for enjoyment and not as a symbolic celebration as in earlier times, therefore a degree of mobility of the plants was desirable. Some of the flowers he included in this catalogue were already being employed decoratively in 'knoted beds' in grander and more spacious locations: heartsease, bachelor's buttons and marigolds, for example. The housewife is reminded to collect plants from the wild and introduce them into the garden if necessary or to consider the wild harvest.

The nature of flowers dame Physick doth shew,
She teacheth them all to be known to a few.
To set or to sow, or else sowne to remove
How that should be practised, learne if ye lov.

Seedes and Herbes for the Kitchen

Here we find an endearing and informative list of what Tusser considered necessary for the kitchen, yet many had multiple contemporary uses.

Avens: An aromatic antiseptic and tonic, the roots of which Tusser would know as a clove flavouring for ale or wine to inhibit sourness

Betanie: (Betony). A cure-all from monastic times, and a plant endowed with considerable power against evil spirits.

Bleet or Beets: White or yellow. No doubt what today would be considered to be the unrefined mangel wurzel and beetroot, and then used as a pot herb. Although John Evelyn considered bleet to be Good King Henry.

Bloodwort: Probably danewort or elder and yet no culinary qualities have been applied to this fetid plant. The smoke from the ash was believed to drive away serpents and venomous beasts. Called danewort, this plant, believed to be *Sambucus ebulus*, trailed a little bit of Anglo-Saxon plant lore into the sixteenth century; they believed it sprang up wherever blood of the marauding Danes was spilled.

Buglas: Bugloss (*Anchusa officinalis*), which a century later John Evelyn said had become confused with borage *(Borago officinalis)*, but Tusser was quite clear as he lists borage separately.

Burnet: A fragrant herb grown for its flavour. Later Bacon recommended it to be undertrodden to perfume the air.

Burrage: Borage was the great giver of courage. Sometimes boiled as a pot herb and the cucumber-flavoured leaves eaten fresh and added to beverages.

Cabbage remove in June: Here Tusser was reminding his readers to transplant the brassica seedlings to encourage good heads.

Clarie: (Clary). Believed to have been introduced into England about 1562, and certainly included in the later editions of *Five Hundred Points.* Gerard described it also.

Coleworts: Brassicas of various sorts, as pot herbs and pickled with vinegar to make a kind of sauerkraut.

Endive: Then a newly introduced plant in Tusser's day (*Cichorium endiva*).

Fennell: Also known in Tusser's day as fenkel, for its strong anise flavour and for its almost mythical power to restore sight, a belief inherited from the Ancient World.

French Mallows: Mallows or cheeses, from the shape of the edible fruit, was a plant commonly used as a vegetable. Flowers used fresh, or dried with others, with sugar or honey made a conserve.

French Saffron: Set in August. The flowers were collected in September.

Langdebiefe: (Langue de Boeuf). A variety of bugloss or anchusa used to make an ordinary pottage together with strawberry leaves, violets and marigolds, added to oatmeal. The roots were bound to varicose veins to relieve the pain.

Leekes remove in June: A gardening note.

Lettis remove in May: Another instruction.

Longwort: Known also at the time as sage of Jerusalem and probably *Pulmonaria officinalis*. It was eaten with meat and eggs, and called 'sage' together with several other plants.

Liverwort: Probably *Hepatica* sp., the liver-shaped leaves of which suggested its medicinal purpose.

Marigolds often cut: Tusser knew the remontant quality of the marigold, the leaves and flowers fresh or dried were ingredients of broths and salads. Petals added colour to food as a substitute for saffron, and were used for syrups and conserves, and in cosmetic waters.

Mercurie: Mercury. A *Chenopodium* of which several were used as a spinach-like vegetable, or eaten uncooked.

Mints at all times: The ubiquitous mints in their fecund forms were obviously known to Tusser as invasive and perennial plants. In the kitchen the clean sharp flavour was a favourite and used to permeate vinegars and sauces and to distil as a cordial.

Nep: Catnep or catmint. The small leaves, dried or fresh, made catmint tea, widely imbibed before the advent of tea or coffee.

Onions from December to March: Onions were, as now, a good-keeping winter vegetable and flavouring agent.

Orache or arach redde and white: Forms of *Atriplex hortensis*, most popular in the white, or green form and used as a spinach-like pot herb.

Patience: Herb patience or monk's rhubarb is a little-recorded herb from Tudor times, used for the sorrel-like flavour of its leaves as a pot herb.

Perceley: Parsley, of which two or three forms were known, both plain and curled of leaf. Hamburg or parsnip-rooted parsley is not recorded from this period; however, two centuries later it was commonly sold in the London markets.

Peneriall: Pennyroyal, or the more descriptive name pudding grass suggests its employment as stuffing for hog meat together with honey. Henry Lyte says that it was used to sweeten tainted water.

Primrose: Primrose flowers and root infused made a sedative tisane, primrose tea, which Gerard says 'drunk in the month of May is famous for curing the phrencie'. Primrose pottage, a combination of almonds, honey and primrose flowers was a spring dessert.

Rosemary in the Springtime to growe south or west: Here Tusser reveals that he understands that rosemary prefers a sunny sheltered spot.

Sage red and white: White sage was no doubt *Salvia officinalis*; the red-leaved sort today we know as purple sage. Leaves were used from ancient days as an adjunct to fatty meats, and the flowers added to broths, pottage and sallets.

English saffron set in August:	A cultural reminder for the widely cultivated food colouring.
Summer saverie:	Summer savory, the annual provided tasty, somewhat peppery leaves, to combine with thyme and marjoram to season fowl or veal. (Tusser lists marjoram only as a strewing herb.)
Sorrell:	Sorrel. Used as a pot herb or sallet.
Spinage:	Spinach. A pot herb, a constituent of broths and stews.
Suckerie:	Chicory. Apparently little grown, and then used as a root vegetable, together with others to mask its dry somewhat bitter flavour.
Tanzie:	Tansy. The spicy flavour of the chopped leaves was a substitute for nutmeg and cinnamon. Gerard confirms that Tansy Pudding was served in Lent.
Time:	Thyme, even in Tusser's day, was a universal flavouring for stuffings, pickles and soups.
Violets of all sorts:	These would include heartsease and the flowers were candied or made into a syrup used as a sweetmeat.
Winter saverie:	Winter savory, the evergreen, was pounded and combined with breadcrumbs 'to give it quick relish' as Gerard puts it.

Tusser then continues with repetitive lists that throw some light on to the culinary variation: Herbs and Rootes for Sallets and Sauce; Herbs and Rootes to Boile or to Butter. Additional flavourings such as capers, Lemmans (lemons), Olives, Orengis (oranges), Rise (rice) and Sampire he mentions with an accompanying couplet.

These buie with the penie,
or looke not for anie.

Herbs to Strewe

We have seen already that strewing plants on floors was a common practice. 'Strewing Herbes of all Sorts' included fragrant flowering plants, such as lavender, roses, violets, daisies, primroses and cowslips as well as the basil by which he no doubt means wild basil. *Calamintha*, as the culinary basil we know as such, was introduced from India some twenty years later. During mid-summer he recommends that wormwood be gathered for strewing.

While wormwood hath seed, get handful or twaine,
to save against March to make flea to refraine;
Where chamber is sweeped, and wormwood is strowne
no flea for his life dar abide to be known.
What saver is better (if physicke be true)
for places infected, than wormwood and rue.
It is as a comfort for hart and the braine
and therefore to have it, it is not in vaine.

Appointed strewers lived at Court at one time and we read that Mary Dowle was the Strewer of Herbes in Ordinary to His Majesty James II. For his coronation, detailed instructions were issued: blue cloth for the procession to walk along 'amounting to 1220 yards which cloth is strewed with nine Baskets full of sweet herbs and flowers by the Strewer of Herbes in Ordinary to His Majesty, assisted by six women two to a Basket, each basket containing two Bushels'.

STILL ROOMS

Perhaps one of the most important duties of a housewife was to ensure some means of doctoring to the sick, easing labour pains, soothing festering wounds, comforting teething babies, cleaning and preparing food. Most of the better houses possessed a still room (or distilling room) where herbs and flowers from the garden and surrounding countryside were transformed into scented waters or medicinal tinctures. Skilled maids or the chatelaine organized the work, which reached a peak during the summer months, as herbs were prepared for storing and using in an array of cosmetics, mouth washes, pomades, pomanders, aromatic vinegars, perfumed soap, perfumed candles and scented tobacco. The Elizabethans had a lovely host of aromatic materials available, from the markets or the apothecary's shop, and in London from Bucklersbury Market. Shakespeare made Falstaff describe the scented fops as 'Smelling as sweet as Buckleberry in simpling time'. Odoriferous materials new to England then were balsam of Peru, vanilla, gum, tacamahac and other exotic aromatic materials such as neroly and tuberose, preparations brought home first from the Levant by the Crusaders for their wives and mistresss. No wonder that Tudor Society embraced such extravagances as scented gloves and shoes; it is said the Earl of Oxford who first returned from Italy, set the fashion in motion, with his scent bags, gloves and scented jerkin.

Some ladies are reputed to have slept in their scented gloves to keep their hands soft and alluring! Chambers and apartments were scented with pot pourri or by burning home-made incense and aromatic cones or pastilles and fragrant herbs were strewn over the floor, their aromatic oils released by trampling feet; flower and herb waters were sprinkled in rooms and over clothing in closets and chests.

Household still-room receipt books record numberless ideas and formulas, some contributed by friends and families passed these down from one generation to the next, each adding contemporary ideas and new recipes. Many included remedies for illness, and 'to gladden the heart' or 'to comfort the brain'; most of the old recipes seem vague, recommending to use 'as much as you think fit', but Elizabethan ladies would have been familiar with the plants they were using, just as today we understand what is meant by 'a knob of butter'.

Tisanes

Scented teas were made for medicinal purposes, or purely as an enjoyable beverage, from an infusion or *tisane* of leaves and/or flowers. Horehound, sage, mullein, marshmallow or raspberry leaves relieved pulmonary and respiratory complaints. Peppermint, caraway, pennyroyal, catnep, melilot and marjoram calmed an upset stomach and relieved indigestion. For headaches meadowsweet, feverfew, lavender, lemon balm, ground ivy (known as gill tea), woodruff, melilot, lady's bedstraw and pennyroyal were favourites. Gerard even recommended that 'A Garland of pennyroyal made and worne about the head is of great force against the swimming of the head and the paine and giddiness thereof'.

Combinations of various herbs were made and no doubt mothers and grandmothers each had their firm recommendations. For 'runny tummy', several herbs could be associated such as mullein, nettle, comfrey, plantain and betony. To induce sleep tisanes of chamomile, hop, lemon balm, mullein flowers, violet flowers and lime flowers were taken and little bags of crushed dried leaves of the same plants were placed on the bolster of the bed, or pillows were filled with drowsy-making herbs. Herb pillows had to be replenished with sweet-smelling dried plant material every few weeks, and were an extension of the Medieval practice of stuffing sweet grasses and aromatic plants into mattresses to combat insects and vermin.

Culinary delights

Honey was esteemed as a sweetener and flowers served the same purpose, often made into a syrup.

Pounds or pints of flower petals were required for the recipes, and flowers were candied and preserved for later use. Markham explains the garnishing of dishes with crystallized flowers: gillyflowers, mallows, cowslips, primroses, roses, violets, bugloss, rosemary and St Mary golds were used popularly.

Fragrant smoke

Strong smelling aromatics were burned effectively to rid the air of pestilence and foul odours. Bay leaves, juniper, aromatic resins, all served this purpose and there is little evidence of herbs as such being employed in this way. Incense cones or fragrant pastilles were burned to sweeten the air indoors, while imports from the Middle East included considerable quantities of Levant Paste which contained many more exotic eastern fragrances. All these would be burned in a metal chafing dish, or placed near to a fire or flame to encourage the warmth to volatilize the fragrant oils. Small metal boxes with lids decoratively perforated, known as cassolettes were filled with such scented pastes which, when set in a warm place, allowed the scent to pervade the room. Further, lovely silver vessels, called pomos were put appropriately into little charcoal burners (willow charcoal for preference) to simmer the contents of rose water, herbs and spices. The rose water was replenished from time to time.

> *Take a glassful of Rose Water, Cloves well beaten to a powder, a penny weight; then take the fire panne and make it red hot in the fyre, and put thereon of the said Rose water with the sayd powder of Cloves making it so consume little by little, but the rose water must be muskt, and you shall make a parfume of excellent good odour.*
>
> A Queen's Delight (*1665*)

Many of these scented conceits were made in family still rooms, some ingredients being purchased from the apothecary's shop or the local market or from itinerant pedlars or chapmen. Sometimes a gum-based receipt would be moulded into the form of a little bird or animal, a flower or fish, gilded and then lighted at one point to burn slowly.

Fragrant powders

The tradition of containing fragrant powders with little sachets began in fifteenth-century Italy and spread quickly to other European countries. Some powdered herb root such as sweet rush, orris (*Iris florentina*), or spikenard acted as a perfume fixative and was added to dried crushed leaves of verbena, lavender, marjoram, mugwort, rose petals, jasmine flowers, balm, clary, woodruff, yarrow, lavender cotton, bay and chamomile flowers and many others, together with fragrant woods. Where the sachets were to be used for their insecticidal properties, lemon thyme, southernwood, rue, wormwood, fleabane and elecampane root would be included.

Scented powders sprinkled among linen clothes and furs was an ancient universal practice and it was during the fifteenth and sixteenth centuries that the practice developed of tying flowers of lavender and rose and sprigs of rosemary, sage, and other fragrant plants into clothing. Held in caps as William Turner recommended lavender and sweet smelling flowers were fastened inside capes, or tucked into hose; they all served as deodorants however decorative. Whenever John Danvers, whose brother had founded the Botanic Garden at Oxford, left his home in Chelsea he first went into the garden to rub his hat in the hyssop bush — a lovely practice.

TO MAKE A SWEET POWDER FOR BAGS

Take leaves of Rose leave dryed two handfuls, or Orris four ounces of dryed Marjoram one handful, Cloves one ounce, Benjamin two ounces, of white Sanders and yellow of each one ounce; beat all these into a glass powder, then put to it of Muse a dram, a civet half a dram, and of Ambergreece half a dram, then put them into a Taffety Bag and use it.

Gervase Markham, The English Housewife (*1625*)

Pot Pourri

Literally translated this French word means 'rotten pot' and here is the clue to its origin. At one time it was a stock pot stew of food, plants (which today would be classed as vegetables) and flowers such as marigolds and violets that were included. Apothecaries sold off their redundant dried flowers and leaves and other by-products of their trade. The stewed concoction resembled a flower pickle which, with the addition of spices and fixatives, could be preserved for long periods by moistening with brandy or some other spirit. When in the sixteenth century, spices and other fragrant materials became more widely available, the 'rotten pot' took on a far more sensual appeal. It could be pressed into stiff layers and allowed to dry, to be moistened and revived later, or it could be reserved in closed containers to retain the rich aromas and opened only when required to scent a room. The sad colours seem to have been unimportant. Only as time passed were brightly coloured dried flowers like marigold and nigella included.

MOIST POT POURRI

A moist pot pourri has a far stronger scent than its dry counterpart, and in the damp houses with beaten floors the stronger sharper scents were appreciated more. Although visually less attractive, the moist product is far longer lasting and there are (tall!) stories of replenishing moist pot pourri to keep it for 50 years! During the early seventeenth century, a way was developed of making moist pot pourri by fermenting rose and other scented petals in a large crock with alternate layers of flowers and bay salt. Thus a far stronger and longer lasting mixture was produced. Over the years this became known as 'sweet jar'. Ladies developed their own family recipes, adding spices such as nutmeg, cloves, mace, cassia and retained the mixture in large jars, or as the years went by in decorative purpose-made pot pourri jars and caskets with perforated lids.

DRY POT POURRI

On the other hand dry pot pourri was a far more *ad hoc* affair; dried, scented petals and aromatic leaves would be added as the summer progressed. Nutmeg and cloves were grated into it and some orris root or sweet rush root added as a fixative. Dried citrus peel, sassafras, pine needles or even vanilla also went into it, the whole mass being mixed frequently.

Writing in 1594 Sir Hugh Platt in *Delights for Ladies* gave precise instructions for selecting and drying roses: 'You must in rose-time make choice of such roses as are neither in bud, nor full blowne' and he describes the method of drying in sand in much the same way as is accomplished today '. . . and thus you may have rose leaves and other flowers to lay about your basons, windows, etc. all winter long'. He then suggests a delightful way to learn your herbs; 'Also this secret is very requisite for a good simplifier, because he may dry the leaf in his herbal with the simple [herb] which it representeth, whereby he may easily learne to know the names of all simples which he desireth'.

STREWING

Strewing of herbs remained a necessity rather than a refinement and apparently Queen Elizabeth preferred meadowsweet above all other plants. Gerard tells us that it 'far exceeds all other strewing herbs, to deck up houses to strew in chambers, halls and banqueting houses (garden building) in summer time; for the smell thereof makes the heart merry and delighteth the senses: neither doth it cause headache as some other sweet smelling herbs do'. It was the romantic and frivolous Tudors who sprinkled flowers among the strewn rushes, marigolds, pinks and other gillyflowers, cowslips, hawthorn blossom, honeysuckle, mullein and columbine.

Amulets

Some aromatics provided preventative measures taken against infection, the Plague in particular, as a poem from 1625 shows.

One with a piece of tasseld well tarr'd Rope
Doth with that nosegay keep himself in hope;
Another doth a wispe of worme-wood pull
And with great Judgement crams his nostrils full;
A third takes off his socks from's sweting feete,
And makes them his perfume alongst the streete;
A fourth hath got a pownc'd Pommander box
With worm-wood juice, or sweating of a Fox
Rue steep'd in Vinegar, they hold it good
To chere the scenes, and preserve the blood.

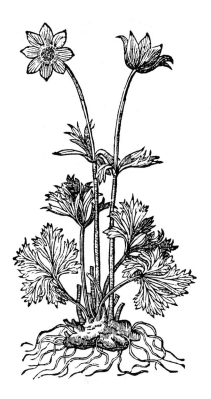

Herbal posies, amulets, pomanders, herb sachets and fragrant beads seem all to have served a dual purpose to provide an aromatic trinket about the person and to protect against disease. From classical times and throughout the Dark Ages we have seen that the carrying of a charm to protect against unknown dangers was a very common practice, so an element of magic accompanied the amulets of the Tudor period. Uppermost in intent seems to have been the superstition that the scented bauble would attract infection, destroy it and transpose it into a spirit-strengthening symbol. Habitually, therefore, some amulet was worn around the neck, resting near the heart. Ingredients could be combined and retained in some scented gum or perfume fixative powder, the imprecise formula of which encouraged charlatans. (Fifty years later Nicholas Culpeper recommended a concoction of 138 aromatic ingredients.)

The Tudor mind retained the belief in magic so 'Conjurors, bad Physitians, lewd Chirurgians, Melancholick Witches and Coseners' proffered all manner of amulets: periapts of metal or ivory or zenextons of silver with an engraved scorpion and/or serpant. Sometimes the ingredients of these were prepared according to some astrological rule, and pearls, jewels, horn, powdered toad beetles and 'stag's pizzle' and herbs were combined. Typical herbs seem to have been rue, wormwood, rosemary, angelica, yarrow, borage, fennel, bay, juniper, ivy, germander, mint, betony, vervain, lavender (especially *Lavandula stoechas*), marjoram, horehound, saffron and sage.

HERBS IN MEDICINE

Let us turn to Gerard, herbalist of the day, for confirmation of herbal practitioners' prescriptions, many of which are an engaging muddle that only make us squirm. Gerard enlightens us as to a preparation of all-heal he employed in one of his successful treatments of a Mr Edmund Cartwright, 'A Gentleman of Grayes Inn in Holborne', who suffered a chest wound:

I took four handfulls of the herbe stamped, and put them into a pan,
whereunto I added four ounces of Barrowes grease, halfe a pinte of oyle
Olive, wax three ounces, which I boyled into the consumption of the
juyce (which is known when the stuff doth not bubble at all) then did I
straine it, putting it to the fire again, adding thereto two ounces of
Turpentine, the which I suffered to boile a little, reserving the same for
my use, The which I warmed in a saucer, dipping therein small soft
tents, which I put into the wound, defending the parts adjoyning with a
plaster of calcitheos, relented with oyle of roses; which manner of
dressing and preserving I used even untill the wound was perfectly
whole: not withstanding once a day I gave him two spoonfulls of this
decoction following. I tooke of good Claret wine, wherein I boyled a
handfull of the leaves of Solidago Saracenica *or Saracens consound, and*
foure ounces of honey, whereof I gave him in the morning two Spoonefulls
to drinke in a small draught of wine tempered with a little sugar.

A cartouche from the title page of some editions of Gerard's Herbal *(1597) shows simple rectangular raised beds laid out in the fashion of all gardens prior to the fanciful ideas of the Tudors.*

Comfits

Gerard tells us, too, how to candy sea holly, reporting that he brought it into his garden from Langtree Point on the other side of the water from Harwich: 'The roots conditioned or preserved with sugar as hereafter followeth are exceeding good to be given to old and aged people that are consumed and withered with age, and which want natural moisture: they are also good for all sorts of people, nourishing and restoring the aged, and amending the defects of nature in the younger'.

Self-heal

'It groweth in moist medowes by the sides of ditches and likewise in fertile fields that are somewhat moist, almost every where; especially in Kent' (where he had done some of his botanizing). So Gerard wrote of clownes wound-wort or all-heale, clownes all-heale or the husbandman's wound-wort.

> *. . . For being in Kent about a Patient, it chanced that a poore man in mowing of Peason did cut his leg with a sithe wherein hee made a wound to the bones, and withall very large and wide, and also with great effusion of bloud; the poore man crept unto this herbe, which he bruised with his hands and tied a great quantitie of it unto the wound with a piece of his shirt, which presently stanched the bleeding, and ceased the paine, insomuch that the poore man presently went to his daies worke againe, and so did from day to day, without resting one day until he was perfectlly whole; which was accomplished in a few daies.*

Self help indeed which perhaps explains why today the plant is known as self-heal! Gerard then enlightens us as to the preparation.

Smoking

When Sir Walter Raleigh initiated the habit of smoking tobacco in his pipe, the concept of inhaling smoke was not new. In the past the patients had been encouraged to lean over a brazier of burning herbs in order to inhale their 'virtues'. Herb tobaccos and tobacco mixtures (which contained no tobacco at all) were often homemade from such herbs as yarrow, betony, tansy, thyme and coltsfoot. Rosemary, chamomile, poppy petals, lavender, sage, elderflowers and comfrey have all been added to tobacco or used in various combinations of pleasing consistency that burns gently.

Smoking as a concept was practised in the Ancient World according to Pliny and narcotics like opium are of ancient use. As the written word confirms practice it can be assumed with considerable certainty that 'inhaling' was commonly believed to clear the head. Richard Bancke's *Herbal* (1525) states: 'To cleanse the brain of superfluous humours, take a quantity of maces and chew them well . . . hold them there awhile, and that shall loose the fumosity of humours that rise up to the brain, and purge the superfluity of it'. Although not necessarily for their ineffectiveness, as we shall see, synthetic products dominated later.

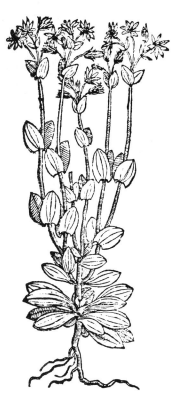

THE STUDY OF PHYSIC PLANTS

One of the activities that runs like a thread through the years from the monasteries to the College gardens was the study of plants. Formal University learning had been implemented by Physic or Botanic Gardens at some European medical schools, but the first to be started in England was at Oxford: formalities completed, the foundation stone was laid on the afternoon of 25 July 1621.

As part of the School of Medicine it was founded by Henry Danvers, Earl of Danby, on five acres of land leased from Magdalen College. Progress was slow during the first twenty years, partly due to the Civil War, and because the land needed to be raised against winter flooding from the river Cherwell which washed its southern and eastern boundaries. During this time a stout 14-ft wall was built to enfold much of the land, and still stands today enclosing the geometrically laid-out beds of the original plan. Inigo Thomas designed the sturdy main gate, through which visitors to the garden pass today.

Jacob Brobart the Elder was the first *Horti Praefectus* (garden supervisor) appointed in 1641. A former local inn keeper by trade, but no doubt well versed in his simples, he published the first *Catalogue of Plants* in the garden in 1648. It included 1600 plants, only 600 of the British natives, from which the interest in introduced plants can be seen.

New and wondrous plants

By this time, numerous new plants had been imported to enrich gardens, but the herbs or physic plants remained the mainstay. Also it is highly probable that only the botanical *cognoscenti* acquired the curios and certainly during the Civil Wars the people would turn to their herbs. Throughout the first half of the seventeenth century, garden design remained static, inhibited by the political unrest, but the plantsmen continued their enthusiastic exchange of plants and augmented their collections and knowledge.

Parkinson, that great amasser of plants was preparing his *Paradisus* and John Tradescant the Elder was roaming Europe from the Arctic Circle to the Mediterranean in search of plants. He and his son, another John, were listing, describing, introducing and growing plants from the New World. The younger Tradescant made three journeys in 1637, 1642 and 1654, in search of new decorative plants. One of the main attractions of the American plants must have rested in their later flowering than the English spring lovelies: monardas, eupotorium and the Virginian strawberry (*Fragaria virginiana*) augmented the list of herbs. Wild strawberries had been grown since the tenth century and Tusser knew them, the tangled network of stems giving the plant its name from the verb 'to strew'. The arrival of larger fruited kinds excited the herbalists who interpreted the Doctrine of Signatures, whereby a plant revealed its purpose by its form, as holding a power to cure ailments of the blood (menstrual bleeding, wounds and the blood flux).

Many plants arriving at this time were novelties, sold at higher prices, just as the potato remained a botanical curio, although Sir Walter Raleigh had brought it back at the end of the 1580s (together with the tobacco-smoking habit). When Gerard's portrait appeared on the frontispiece of his *Herball* in 1597 he was depicted holding the flower of the potato plant, but it was by no means well known until the eighteenth century.

Joyful News out of a New Found World

In the late 1570s — authorities vary between 1577 and 1580 — John Frampton translated into English a Seville physician's account of plants brought to Europe from the recently discovered West Indies. The title was *Joyful News out of a New Found World* (1569 and 1571). Nicholas Monardes described the great riches that came from America in 'every yere one hundred shippes laden', with gold, silver, precious stones, pearls, dyes, woods, skins and sugar all being described and many plants of 'great medicinall vertues'. Balsams, gums, fruits, oils, in addition to officinal plants themselves were among the unbelievable wonders that arrived in Europe.

The book is popularly quoted as displaying the first illustration of the tobacco plant, with much adulation for its curative powers as a healing plant and one to 'adornate' gardens. The prescription for the ointment of tobacco read: 'Take a pounde of the freshe leaves of the sayde Hearbe stampe them, and mingle them with newe Waxe, Rosine, sommon oyle of each three ounces, let them boyle altogether, until the Juice of Nicotiane be consumed, then add thereto three ounces of Venise Turpentine, straine the same through a linen cloth, and keepe in Pottes to your use'. Strangely it seems today, tobacco was recommended also for shortness of breath, 'to take the smoke in at the mouth'. The popularity of John Frampton's translation was as much an expression of the quest for the new and curious as a genuine search for knowledge. Economic botany, and herbal practice on the one hand and gardening for pleasure and the development of horticulture on the other were coming to a parting of the ways.

An idealized garden of the Stuart period, secluded and laid out in a more imaginative design. The gardener demonstrates his 'outlandish plant' of Fritillaria imperialis. *Such a design probably offers the first historical reference for the decorative formal herb garden.*

III

ENGLISH HERBALS

I judge that flowers of lavender quilted in a cap and worne are good for all diseases of the head that come from a cold cause and that they comfort the brain very well.

William Turner, New Herball, (1551)

Herbals are considered to be works which set out to describe the practical uses of plants in a non-scientific way. Over the centuries they afford a glimpse into contemporary attitudes and beliefs and often lag behind any botanical understanding because they confirmed practice and were designed for the common people. The description 'herbal' continued to be used into the nineteenth century, when in fact it was applied to what had become a medical botany. Exciting advances in printing techniques and a hungry curiosity for illustrations of highly coloured and richly scented plants for the decorative garden, submerged the popular household herbal during the eighteenth and nineteenth centuries. So that by the 1830s *The Gardens Chronicle* in answer to a correspondent could say 'We do not know what you mean by a Herbal. The term is disused'.

The apparent gap between the Anglo-Saxon manuscripts and the first printed herbals in English appears because incunabula were in Latin and were produced mainly in Germany and Italy. What was produced in England amounted to manuscript treatises, many of them copies of Continental works and lacking in originality. Any originality was based upon hearsay or, occasionally, personal findings and depended quite forcefully upon astrological ideas. Instructions for accompanying Pater Nostas or Ave Marias to the gathering of herbs assumed importance, and clouded the purpose of the herbal proper with an airy vagueness. Eleanour Sinclair Rohde researched the manuscripts of the Medieval period and records some of them in *The Old English Herbals* (1922).

The Which is Called an Herbal

The earliest English printed herbal came in 1525, 'Imprynted by me Rycharde Banckes'. In block letters, this little book proclaimed 'Here begynneth a newe mater, the whiche sheweth and treateth of ye vertues and proprytes of herbes, the which is called an Herball'. Conjecture suggests it to be a garnering from some Medieval manuscript describing the plants themselves and eulogizing upon their virtues. Rosemary was considered to raise the spirits when the powdered flowers were bound to the right arm; it was recommended for scenting linen in chests and when boiled in white wine as a wash would ensure that 'thou shall have a fayre face'. Several imprints more or less contemporary followed this first 'Herbal' in English.

The Grete Herball

First published in 1526, *The Grete Herbal* made no claim to originality and in fact was a translation of a well-known French herbal. What it can claim to be is the first illustrated book on plants, for which read herbs, to be published in England and to be in the vernacular. England, although lagging behind the mainland Europe in the progress of printing, was together with Italy, leading the way by publishing in the vernacular for an unschooled public. Printed in block letter by Peter Treveris, 'dwellynge in the sygne of the wodows' at Southwark, it ran to several editions over the ensuing 35 years. The extended title read in part. 'The grete herball whiche geveth parfyt knowlege and understandyng of all maner of herbes to there gracyous vertues whiche god hath ordeyned for our prosperous welfar and helth . . .'.

WILLIAM TURNER (*c.* 1508/10–1568)

The first original work on plants to be written in English in the sixteenth century was William Turner's *New Herball.* He was the first Englishman who appears to have studied plants in a reasoned manner, thus this book and his other works have gained for him the accolade 'Father of British Botany'.

A clergyman, born in Morpeth, Northumberland some time between 1508 and 1510, Turner was educated at what is now Pembroke College, Cambridge. He was closely associated with the Reformation and on account of his strong Protestant principles fled to the Continent of Europe when the climate of the English Court was unfavourable to him. During the reign of Henry VIII his writing was banned and he suffered imprisonment for preaching without call, but the pendulum swung in his favour during the reign of Edward VI and he became Dean of Wells in Somerset, although it was not long before he scurried back across the Channel. His travels during the periods of his exile offered wide opportunities for meeting the leading botanists of the time, and of gardening in reasonable peace — he had gardens in both Cologne and Weissenburg. In earlier exile he studied medicine at Bologna under a renowned botanist Luca Ghini for physic plants upheld both medicine and botany at that time. Turner's botanical work has remained, his religious writings not so. One book published early in his career (1548) was entitled *The names of herbes in Greke, Latin, Englishe, Duche and French wyth the commune names that Herbaries and Apothecaries use, gathered by William Turner.* Herein lies the clue to Turner's general intention, expanded in the later work, of writing about the plants the common people knew.

In the various editions of the *Herball,* English names for plants were not the only ones used; Turner coined more, some of which have persisted as vernacular names. For example, toadflax, willow herb, wood sorrel and bitter sweet. There were those who abhorred the idea claiming that '. . . every man nay every old wyfe will presume, not without the wordre of many to practyse Phisick'. Turner's reply throws light on contemporary practice; he asked 'How many surgianes and apothecaries are there in England which can understand Plini in Latin or Galen and Dioscorides'? The physicians, he pointed out, relied upon the apothecaries and they, in turn, upon the herb women who gather the herbs. By presenting his work in English, Turner sought to enlighten the practitioners themselves and mitigate malpractice.

Steven Mierdman, a Protestant refugee from Antwerp, printed the first part of the *Herball* in 1551. The second part appeared about ten years later, printed in Cologne by Arnold Brickman, delayed because of Turner's enforced exile. Finally in 1568 the year of Turner's death, a complete edition was printed at Cologne comprising Parts I, II and III. Dedicated to Queen Elizabeth I, William Turner explains in the preface that he 'wente into Italy and into diverse partes of Germany to knowe and se the herbes for my selfe', demonstrating again that numerous commonly used physic plants were, in fact, central and southern European natives. At Wells, he 'did diligentlye taste certaine aromatic herbes' that were not easily identified.

Eleanour Sinclair Rohde in *The Old English Herbals* remarks on the 'accurate observations and careful descriptions' of Turner being reminiscent of the Saxon herbals. Scholarship of the intervening years, as we have seen, had been dependent upon copying and repetition, and was always related to the Mediterranean flora which the classical writers had described. With Turner much superstition is discounted, and folklore unrecorded, although rural customs are described, and his detailed and original description of the plants as 'simples' reveals his regard for them.

He refuted the old-world dependence upon pupettes fashioned from mandrake root: 'They are so trymmed of crafty thieves to mocke the poore people withall and robs them both of theyr wit and theyr money', but the hoax continued as part of plant superstition and we find Gerard recording it 40 years later.

HENRY LYTE (1529–1607)

In 1578 an English version of the *Cruydeboeck* was published, freely translated and amended by Henry Lyte, gentleman. He was the first 'amateur' botanist to offer his observations. His work appears to have been developed from the L'Ecluse French

Henrie Lyte Efq; the eldeſt ſon of Iohn Lyte Efq; firſt ma: Agnes ỹ da: of Kail way of Cullunton Efq: his 2 wife was Frances ỹ da: of Iohn Typtoſt a Citizen of Londō. his 3 wife was Dorothy ỹ da: of on Iohn Gouer. He died at the age of 78 and was buried in ỹ North Ile at Charl ton Mackarell An: 1607.

Henry Lyte was the first amateur botanist to write a herbal in English. His book A Niewe Herball or Historie of Plantes *proved to be immensely popular. It was an up-dated version of the European* Cruydeboeck *with numerous additions and personal observations relating to English plants.*

translation, with additional information gleaned from William Turner and notes derived from other sources. What is remarkable here is that his own observations were incorporated, e.g. 'Solomon's Seal growethe very plentifully at Haredye Wood by Ashewith in the fosse way beyond Shepton Mallett in Somersett'. (This must have been *Polygonatum odoratum.*) Lyte lived in Somerset from whence he dedicated his book to his Queen 'from my poore house at Lytescarie within your Majesties countie of Somersett, the first day of Januarie MDLXXVIII'. Woodcuts originally made for Fuchs and owned by Plantin's publishing house in Antwerp were augmented by 30 original ones and the full title ran *A Niewe Herball or Histoire of Plantes: wherein is contayned the whole discourse and perfect descriptions of all sorts of Herbes and Plants: their divers and sundry kindes; their straunge Figures, Fashions and Shapes; their Names, Natures, Operations and Ventures, and that not onely of those which are here growing in our Countrie of Englande, but of all others also of forrayne Realmes, commonly used*

The ancient manor house of Lytes Cary in Somerset, where Henry Lyte gardened and wrote his book. Today it is administered by the National Trust and is the only surviving home of an Elizabethan writer of a herbal.

in Physicke; First set foorth in the Doutche or Almaigne tongue, by that learned D Rembert Dodoens, Physition to the Emperour: And nowe first translated out of French into English by Henry Lyte Esquyer. Fortunately the work has become known as, simply, A Niewe Herball. Produced in black letter in London, by John Norton — printer, bookseller and publisher of The Queen's Arms in St Paul's Churchyard, and an Alderman of London, A Niewe Herball proved to be a 'best seller'. It is credited with being Edmund Spenser's source of information on plants and the inspiration for his 'Aprill Eclogue' in Shepheardes Calendar.

John Aubrey, writing in the seventeenth century said Henry Lyte 'had a pretty good collection of plants for that age, some few whereof are yet alive'. Correspondence of 1860 records 'There is said to have been a botanic garden at Lytes Cary in Elizabeth's time, but I have not been able to make out from the tenants whether any peculiar plants remain, so as to guess the site'. Today the ancient manor house of Lytes Cary is administered by the National Trust, the river Cary from which it takes its name skirts its boundary. Only for five years during the 1580s Lyte took a London house. Otherwise he dwelt in Somerset and dedicated himself to his collection of plants, and his writing. As an antiquary he believed that the British were the direct descendants of the Trojans and wrote *The Light of Britain* to prove it, which he presented to Queen Elizabeth I on the day she attended St Paul's to give thanks for England's victory over the Spanish fleet.

A barber surgeon and enthusiastic gardener, John Gerard is famous as the compiler of the Herball *(1597). Born in Nantwich, Cheshire, Gerard was closely involved with the leading plantsmen and doctors of London and he had responsibility for the College of Physicians Physic Garden.*

JOHN GERARD (1545–1612)

John Newton, who had printed *A Niewe Herball* was the Queen's printer, and warmed by the success of the publication commissioned one Dr Priest to translate Dodoens' last work *Stirpium Historia Pemptades* (1583) from Latin into English. Tradition claims that the good doctor died before the work was accomplished, and that John Gerard acquired the material which formed the basis of his famous herbal. Dr Priest and two of his contemporary London physicians constituted a Committee of the London College of Physicians to consider a section of a proposed pharmacopoeia. At the same time (*c.* 1588–96), Gerard was curator of the College Physic Garden, and, opportunist that he was, took over the work on the book, only to realize his inability to cope with the Latin (for he was a simple gardener) and, after rearranging the order of the herbs, to match up the plates and text. Evidence emerges of considerable bitterness and acrimony between Gerard and L'Obel who was brought in to add corrections and it seems the book *The Herball or General Historie of Plants* was hastily published in 1597 — probably the printer acting in some desperation! Because Gerard was only a barber-surgeon, responsible for the physic garden, a letter of commendation was appended from Dr Stephen Bredwell testifying to the veracity of Dr Priest's translation: 'Dr Priest for his translation of so much as Dodoens hath hereby left a tombe for his honourable

51

Sepulchre. Master Gerard coming last, but not the least, hath many waies accommodated the whole worke unto our English nation'. At the same time Gerard claimed that 'Dr Priest, one of our London College hath (as I heard) translated the last edition of Dodoens which meant to publish the same, but being prevented by death, his translation likewise perished'. Perhaps we can assume with considerable certainty that in haste the contradiction slipped through.

Time may well have augmented the story, which has played no small part in popularizing the book, which continues to be a Bible to English herbalists, quoted and misquoted *ad infinitum*. Its importance, however, rests much upon the edition of 1633, amended to include 2850 plants by Thomas Johnson, a London apothecary and botanist. By this time, the first botanic garden in England had been founded, although its early years were somewhat unproductive. Johnson himself was born about the time *The Herball* was printed, and served his apprenticeship with William Bell in the parish of St Margaret, Westminster, before establishing his own physic garden and practice about 1626 at the sign of the Red Lion on Snow Hill, in Holborn, London. He died in his thirties of wounds received, as a Royalist, during the Siege of Basing House, Hampshire in September 1644. A coterie of eminent botanists was led by John Goodyer, who assisted Johnson in the revision of *The Herball*, and who contributed to contemporary scholarship by his translation of Dioscorides and Matthiolus with added commentaries.

A capable young man, Thomas Johnson made several trips into the countryside to search for new herbs or to examine them in their natural habitat. 'Herborizing' this came to be called, although Johnson probably knew it as 'simpling'. (A 'simple' was the colloquial name for a useful herb, meaning a single or simple one.) We can imagine Thomas Johnson and a small group of like-minded happy friends setting off into the countryside on horseback or to Margate by sea from London, to find *and record* herbs. We owe some of the earliest records of local plants to these jolly tourists, who perhaps over a jar of ale discussed the identity of plants in days before any reliable system of classification had been established.

The Herball or General Historie of Plants

In appearance the great tome must have seemed surprisingly modern printed in its clear legible Roman type contrasting strongly with the black letter of Henry Lyte's and William Turner's herbals. It affords an extensive insight into Elizabethan awareness of and attitudes towards plants. That society's implicit faith in the power of plants was the product of simple traditions, shared by the great civilizations of the past, that the herbs were effective for both physical and emotional ills. 'The Smell of Basil' Gerard assures us 'is good for the heart . . . it taketh away sorrowfulness', likewise sweet marjoram was for those 'who are given to overmuch sighing'. Not only are the descriptions and observations succinct, but they are tempered by folklore, already ancient at that time. There is lively contemporary comment, some of which reveals the early acquaintance of some exotic plants notably from the Americas. For the first time the 'Virginian Potato' or 'Potato of America' as he knew it, was illustrated and described. 'The temperature and vertues be referred to the common Potato's, being likewise a food, as also a meat for pleasure, equall in goodnesse and wholesomnesse to the same, being either roasted in the embers, or boiled and eaten with oil, vinegar and pepper, or dressed some other way by the hand of a skilled Cooke'. The potato was first grown in England in Lord Burghley's London garden at Cecil House in the Strand, under Gerard's supervision as he was superintendent there. No doubt Master Gerard acquired a tuber or fruit for his own garden in Fetter Lane, Holborn.

As Agnes Arber points out, Gerard's inclusion of the (now) fantastic story of the Barnakle Tree or Goose tree, obliterates any respect for him as a scientist of his day. Whether he included the story to appease his readers, or whether he bore a sneaking suspicion that there was something about the plant kingdom that he still did not quite comprehend, can be only guessed at. As a product of that and previous periods the tale serves to convey the contemporary uncertainties among the unversed. Gerard relates how trees bearing shells, open to produce geese and how shells, attached to ancient shipwrecks develop into sea birds! At the same time Gerard reveals elsewhere that he has no time for charms and 'such foolish toys' and warns his readers against the 'quyacking of unlearned physicians, overbold apothecaries, and foolish women'.

PARADISUS

Amidst the coterie of botanists, apothecaries and gardeners in the first half of the seventeenth century was one who was first and foremost a gardener at heart although he is not remembered so. John Parkinson, citizen and apothecary of London wrote an account of the plants he grew in his garden in so joyous a way conveying a wonder, and the satisfaction that are matched by the title *Paradisi in Sole Paradisus Terrestris* (1629) usually abbreviated to *Paradisus*. A latinized pun on his own name, simultaneously expressing the joy of his perfect pleasure. He captures the loveliness and the colour and the scent, and notes the 'outlandish plants' growing there. Here was the first real gardening book rather than a herbal. Thirteen years later when Parkinson was 73 years of age his *Theatrum Botanicum* was published (1640), the largest herbal in the English language. While it is not for this book that he is first remembered it was undoubtedly a scholarly work. Writing from long experience and with a wealth of herbals, both English and European to review and having been at the centre of an exchange of plant material and information for many years during a fast changing period for the plant world, Parkinson produced an accurate account of medicinal plants of the mid-seventeenth century.

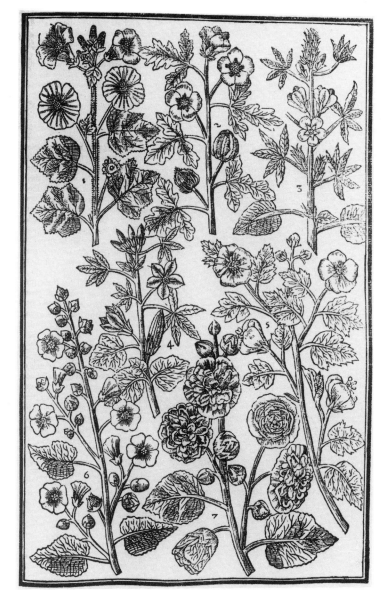

In Paradisus Terrestris *(1629) by John Parkinson seven various mallows and hollyhocks are portrayed. They were grown for their demulcent and emolliant properties, and had been considered to be a sweetmeat by the Romans. Parkinson drew attention to the different forms, some were more decorative than others.*

Of the Goofe tree, Barnakle tree, or the tree bearing Geefe. Chap.167.

Britannica Conchæ anatiferæ.
The breede of Barnakles.

❋ *The defcription.*

HAuing trauelled from the Graffes gro-wing in the bottome of the fenny waters, the woods, and mountaines, euen vnto Libanus it felfe; and alfo the fea, and bowels of the fame: we are arriued to the end of our Hifto-rie, thinking it not impertinent to the conclufi-on of the fame, to end with one of the maruels of this land (we may fay of the world.) The Hi-ftorie whereof to fet foorth according to the woorthines and raritie thereof, woulde not onely require a large and peculiar volume, but alfo a deeper fearch into the bowels of nature, then my intended purpofe wil fuffer me to wade into, my infufficiencie alfo confidered; leauing the hiftorie thereof rough hewen, vnto fome excellent men, learned in the fecrets of nature, to be both fined and refined: in the meane fpace take it as it falleth out, the naked and bare truth, though vnpolifhed. There are founde in the north parts of Scotland, & the Ilands adiacent, called Orchades, certaine trees, whereon doe growe certaine fhell fifhes, of a white colour tending to ruffet; wherein are conteined little liuing creatures: which fhels in time of maturi-tie doe open, and out of them grow thofe little liuing things; which falling into the water, doe become foules, whom we call Barnakles, in the north of England Brant Geefe, and in Lanca-fhire tree Geefe: but the other that do fall vp-on the land, perifh and come to nothing: thus much by the writings of others, and alfo from the mouths of people of thofe parts, which may very well accord with truth.

But what our eies haue feene, and hands haue touched, we fhall declare. There is a fmall Ilande in Lancafhire called the Pile of Foulders, wherein are found the broken peeces of old and brufed fhips, fome whereof haue beene caft thither by fhipwracke, and alfo the trunks or bodies with the branches of old and rotten trees, caft vp there likewife: wheron is found a certaine fpume or froth, that in time breedeth vnto certaine fhels, in fhape like thofe of the muskle, but fharper pointed, and of a whitifh colour; wherein is conteined a thing in forme like a lace of filke finely wouen, as it were togither, of a whitifh colour; one ende whereof is faftned vnto the infide of the fhell, euen as the fifh of Oifters and Muskles are; the other ende is made faft vnto the belly of a rude maffe or lumpe, which in time commeth to the fhape & forme of a Bird: when it is perfectly for-med, the fhel gapeth open, & the firft thing that appeereth is the forefaid lace or ftring; next come the legs of the Birde hanging out; and as it groweth greater, it openeth the fhell by degrees, till at length it is all come foorth, and hangeth onely by the bill; in fhort fpace after it commeth to full maturitie, and falleth into the fea, where it gathereth feathers, and groweth to a foule, bigger then a Maliard, and leffer then a Goofe; hauing blacke legs and bill or beake, and feathers blacke and white, fpotted in fuch maner as is our Magge-Pie, called in fome places a Pie-Annet, which
the

Theatrum Botanicum

He claimed this to be 'more ample and exact than any before', and enumerates some 3800 plants. When he completed *Paradisus*, he told his readers that *A Garden of Simples* would follow 'which will be quiet no longer at home, then that it can bring his master newes of faire weather for the journey'. Was Parkinson really saying that he hoped there would be time to set all his knowledge down, and having done so he would be ready to depart from this world? *Theatrum Botanicum* as it was called, represented the zenith of achievement for herbals, none that appeared later were of equal rank and the gardening world paid far more attention to newly introduced decorative plants and the medical men and the botanists were soon to go their individual ways. Parkinson lived ten more years and was buried at St Martins in the Fields, London, then his own parish church.

Parkinson divided his plants into 17 'Classes or Tribes' revealing a close observation of the growing plant and knowledge of its use in medicine.

1. *Sweet smelling Plants*	10. *Fearnes and Capillary Herbes*
2. *Purging Plants*	11. *Pulses*
3. *Venemous Sleepy and Hurtfull plants and their Counter Poysons*	12. *Cornes*
	13. *Grasses*
4. *Saxifrages*	14. *Marsh Water and Sea Plants and Mosses and Mushroomes*
5. *Vulnerary or Wound Herbs*	
6. *Cooling and Succory Herbs*	15. *The Unordered Tribe*
7. *Hot and Sharpe Biting Plants*	16. *Trees and Shrubbes*
8. *Umbelliferous Plants*	17. *Strange and Outlandish Plants*
9. *Thistles and Thorny Plants*	

'The Unordered Tribe' reveals the humility of the author, admitting he cannot place some plants, or had omitted them (lost his notes!) from the rightful section. Fleabane he says, 'bound to the forehead is a great helpe to cure one of frensie', or 'distilled water of thyme applyed with vinegar of Roses to the forehead easeth the rage of Frensye'. As a slimming drink he recommends 'The powder of the seedes of elder first prepared in vinegar and then in wine halfe a dramme at a time for certaine days together is a meane to abate and consume the fat flesh of a corpulent body and to keep it leane'. He tells us also that 'Queen Elizabeth of famous memorie did more desire meadowsweet than any other sweete herbe to strewe her chambers withall'. The ashes of southernwood mixed with old salad oil will cause a beard to grow or hair on a bald head, and that Solomon's seal, spurge, elecampane, scabious, betony and lupin are all good 'to cleanse the skinne from freckles sunburn and wrinkles'. Pewter, brass or wooden vessels were to be scoured with horsetail, and milk could be strained through goosegrass. To read Parkinson's delightful prose is to step back in time. He accounts for every eventuality, medicinal, household and cosmetic.

Opposite:
Gerard's description of 'The breede of Barnakles' or the Goose Tree from The Herball. *From shells retained by old shipwrecks, birds were said to come and later to grow feathers which identified them as 'bigger than a Mallard, and lesser then a Goose'. While much of Gerard's work elucidates plants, and herbs in particular, he perpetuated some older beliefs especially those for which he had no explanation.*

THE ENGLISH PHYSICIAN

Culpeper's *Herball* belongs to the mid-seventeenth century in more ways than one. It reflects the popular side of medicine, for although Nicholas Culpeper sacrificed much in wealth and reputation to serve the common people — he worked especially in the East End of London — surely he was playing to the gallery, which resulted in the immense popularity of his herbal. The full title of his book first issued in 1649 was *The English Physician or an Astrologo-physical Discourse of the Vulgar Herbs of this Nation Being a Compleat Method of Physic Whereby a man may preserve his body in health; or cure himself being sick for thee pence charge with such things onely as grow in England, they being most fit for English Bodies.* Culpeper was no plantsman, Parkinson had recently produced his *Theatrum Botanicum* (1640), the most comprehensive catalogue of its day, incorporating native northern European and 'outlandish' plants. Culpeper, on the other hand, dabbled in folklore, astrology and the Doctrine of Signatures, while purporting to elucidate the mysteries of plant virtues to the people so that they could treat themselves effectively. Subsequent editions of *The English Physician* appeared in 1653, 1664, 1693, 1695, 1714, 1725, 1733, 1784, 1792, 1802, 1809, 1814 and 1820. Such an impressive demand can only confirm the notoriety of the book, and the willingness of the commoners to accept its premises. It was, in fact, a transposition of the *London Dispensatory* and therefore drew upon Culpeper the fury of the College of Physicians, who three years later attacked with a broadside entitled 'A farm in Spittlefields where all the knick-knacks of Astrology are exposed to open sale'.

Culpeper stemmed from a well-heeled family, but scorned riches and spent freely in the service of others. Born in Ockley, Surrey in October 1616 two weeks after his father's death, Culpeper was brought up an only child with his maternal grandparents at Isfield, Sussex. While at Cambriage studying the Classics, he became engaged but his fiancée was struck by lightning and died just prior to the wedding. Disheartened he left Cambridge, which angered his grandfather and resulted in the loss of financial support from his family. He became apprenticed to an apothecary in St Helens, Bishopsgate, London and when his master died in 1640, he continued the practice, moving it to Red Lion Street, Spitalfields, London, where he established a physic garden, and married a girl named Anne who was to bear him seven children.

THE ART OF SIMPLING

William Cole or Coles, a doctor from Adderbury, Oxfordshire, who settled in Putney, gives us the most delightful insight into the early seventeenth-century attitudes relating to herbs. He sets himself up as an authority in 'simpling' and simultaneously upholds the Doctrine of Signatures, indulges in folklore and fantasies and is one of the few writers who records herbal treatment for animals. Perhaps in a society that depended upon their animals, the horse in particular, and where herbs were very common commodities, no-one had considered recording such matters. In his *Art of Simpling* (1656) he says that the medical profession frequently leaves the identifying of herbs to the apothecaries 'who for the most part are as ignorant as themselves, and rely commonly upon the words of the silly hearb-women, who many times bring them *quid* for *quo*'. (Part of the Apothecaries' Charter had been to try to eliminate such practice, but alas it was far from the perfect world.) It was Cole who was emphatic that the entire walnut represented the human brain. 'Wall-nuts have the perfect signature of the head', he wrote. The shell represented the skull, and when crushed were efficacious for head wounds; further the thin skin that covers the kernel represented 'the thin scales that envelope the brain'. The kernel itself, the very model of the brain, 'resists poysons' and when 'moystned with the quintessence of wine, and laid upon the Crown of the Head it comforts the brain and head mightily'.

A CURIOUS HERBAL

Intrigue surrounded the compilation of the first herbal to be illustrated by a woman so that the title *A Curious Herbal* may suggest Alice in Wonderland, but has ensured notoriety for Elizabeth Blackwell (née Blacherie). While as Wilfred Blunt points out the 500 hand-coloured etchings are of little artistic worth, they are the work of an amateur whose industry has to be admired. Dr Alexander Blackwell, a Scot, seems to have been something of a 'cowboy' printer, not having served an apprenticeship in that trade, and was therefore ruined by the London printers and he languished in a debtor's gaol.

Elizabeth his wife appealed to Sir Hans Sloane and learned that a herbal of medicinal plants are likely to sell, so moved to live near Chelsea Physic Garden and illustrated plants growing there. Toing and froing to her imprisoned husband who completed the descriptive text, *A Curious Herbal* appeared in 1737–39, redeemed the debts and set Dr Blackwell on his way to Sweden where he lost his head on the scaffold for some conspiracy to interfere with the Swedish succession. While working at Chelsea, Elizabeth Blackwell worked closely with Isaac Rand, the Demonstrator of Plants and would certainly have met Miller the Curator. The full descriptive title of her herbal was *A Curious Herbal containing 500 cuts of the most Useful Plants now in use in the Practice of Physic*. Blanche Henry confirms that the *Curious Herbal* 'had the most comprehensive of figures of medicinal plants in any British Book until the publication of William Woodville's *Medical Botany* (1790–95)'. About thirteen years later and during Elizabeth Blackwell's widowhood, Dr Trew of Nurnberg produced an enlarged and edited edition under the name *Herbarium Blackwelliarum* in five volumes (1750–56).

HISTORY OF PLANTS

An eccentric and somewhat irascible character of the mid-eighteenth century was 'Sir' John Hill, who although originally trained as an apothecary became a prodigious and controversial writer on general horticulture and society. Born about 1716 either at Spalding or Peterborough, he can claim to be the author of the first Linnaean flora to be published in England, *History of Plants* (1751). While this was not offered in any way as a herbal it is of interest here as a reminder that the universal introduction of the binominal system and the reasoning behind it came at this time and over the ensuing century transformed the understanding of botany and of the classification of plants, Hill was a little premature in some ways, but no doubt that was part of the man's conceit. His *Family Herbal* or *The British Herbal* (1755) to give it its baptismal name, again embraced the Linnaean system and was one of the first publications to appear after 1753, the accepted date for the inception of modern botanical nomenclature. Herein, the one-time apothecary Hill described his account as of 'all those English Plants, which are remarkable for their virtues, and of the Drugs which are produced by Vegetables of other Countries, with their descriptions and their uses, as proved by experience. Also directions for gathering and preserving roots, herbs, flowers and seeds; the various methods of preserving these simples for present use; receipts for making distilled waters, conserves, syrups, Juleps, draughts etc. etc., with necessary cautions in giving them. Intended for the use of families', in short, a home medical directory, confirming the common knowledge of plants and their employment in the home as part of the housewifery accomplishments at that time.

Confirmation that distilling of herbs was an everyday domestic chore, comes from Hill when he says, 'Few families are without alembic or still . . . with that instrument the simple waters are to be made with no expense beside (except) the fire'. Amongst further writing from Hill came *Herbarium Britannicum* (1769) and *Virtues of British Herbs* (1770) and it was John Hill who first issued *Hortus Kewensis* (1768) the first catalogue of plants cultivated at Kew.

Pehaps understandably Linnaeus's new ideas had a cool reception in England, based as they were upon dividing plants into 24 major classes according to the number of stamens, and each class subdivided as to the number of styles or stigmas. Thus he designated genera, in turn divided into species, and introduced the two-word of binominal system. In spite of the continued use of vernacular names for herbs and indeed for British native plants in general, it is essential, even today, to identify an official plant by its scientific name in order to establish identity with some certainty. English names, as we have seen, frequently distinguish one plant from another according to its use or its natural habitat, and it was 200 years before Linnaeus that William Turner had attempted a simple identification exercise, universally acceptable, by naming every herb in the vernacular, and appending colloquial translated names.

BOTANICUM MEDICINALE

A certain charm attends the plates drawn by Timothy Sheldrake for his herbal *Botanicum Medicinale* published 1759 by the London bookseller John Millan. Previously (*c.* 1756), Sheldrake issued the plates printed on fine paper in threes, for one shilling or coloured for two shillings 'at the sign of the Black boy in the Strand between St Martins Lane and Lancaster-Court.' The engraving was done by Hemmerich, from Nurnberg who worked in London for some years, and are remarkably fine. Each folio depicts the herb and floral dissections and gives details of period of flowering, habitat, part of plant used, description and the virtues, obviously intended as an informative herbal for the common people. Sheldrake admitted to being self-taught to gain 'some little knowledge of medicine' before embarking upon his drawings which set out to record the medicinal plants on the College of Physicians list.

Born in Norwich, he served first as a saddler and then he took over a distilling office, which enforced him to familiarize himself with drugs and botany. For some time his business flourished when he advertised 'cheap, safe and good medicines' but was curtailed when an Act was enforced which prohibited the sale of distilled spirits, in an effort to combat drunkenness. Sheldrake, not being a recognized apothecary, and to whom the Act did not extend, appealed for help to Sir Hans Sloane in an effort to safeguard his livelihood as he had a family to maintain. By 1742 the Sheldrakes had apparently moved to London and work on the *Botanicum Medicinale* plates began.

'English plants are drawn from nature' he claimed, and by the time the work was published in 1759, the printer referred to him as 'the late ingenious T. Sheldrake'. 'Nothing in any language exceeded this Thirty Years laborious Work of which may truly be said that Nature only equals it, every Thing of the Kind, hitherto attempted, being trivial, compared to this inimitable Performance'. — Thus wrote Millan the printer, opposite the Admiralty, Whitehall.

FLORA MEDICA

In many ways in his medical botany of world plants, John Lindsey achieved what William Curtis had envisaged half a century before. *Flora Medica* (1838) proved to represent the final demise of the herbal proper. Fifteen years before Lindley's *Flora Medica*, Thomas Green had produced his *Universal Herbal or Botanical Dictionary* (1824) in which through two volumes he laboriously recorded most of the then known plants as an alphabetical catalogue. However, descriptions, cultivation and observations were arrested by instructions for herbal remedies when applicable. The book was intended, as Green pointed out, for 'the use of the Farmer — the Gardener — the Husbandman — the Botanist — the Florist — the Country Housekeepers in general'. Instructions were included for making herbal tinctures, infusions, syrups, juices, conserves, ointments and distilled waters with the intention of exposing the herbalists' 'trade secrets', and to meet the popular demand for home medicine prevalent at the beginning of the nineteenth century. Natural locations of many herbs, or wild plants as they were becoming, were recorded and much detail of a 'do-it-yourself' nature concerning household use of plants.

Lindley's work on the other hand was far more erudite, certainly not aimed at the husbandmen and housekeepers, but at medical students and their knowledge of worldwide vegetable drugs. An understanding of medicines was developing and there was still much of the earth's richness of plant life to be explored. Lindley wrote 'England is already found to yield species of such powerful action as Hellebore, Henbane, Belladonna, Stromium, Foxglove, Willowbark, Holly leaves, Spurge Laurel, Centaury, Colchicum, Bryony and Ergot . . .' and wondered what other valuable drugs would be discovered. All those he mentioned had by then been proven to be efficacious for the very same complaints to which they had been allied by the old apothecaries.

Dr John Lindley was one of the giants of horticulture and botany of the nineteenth century. His name is inexorably related to that of the (Royal) Horticultural Society which he served with immeasurable influence from 1820 for over 40 years. He is commemorated in the name of the Lindley Library which was established as a Trust once his books and bookcases had been acquired following his death.

A MODERN HERBAL

The decline of the herbal became absolute so that it was almost a century after John Lindley's *Flora Medica* before Maud Grieve's *A Modern Herbal* was published in 1931. Today, despite a tidal wave of books on the subject of herbs which flooded the bookshops during the 1970s and 1980s, her work retains an authority and accuracy to that date that has to be acknowledged. It represents a record of research that had not

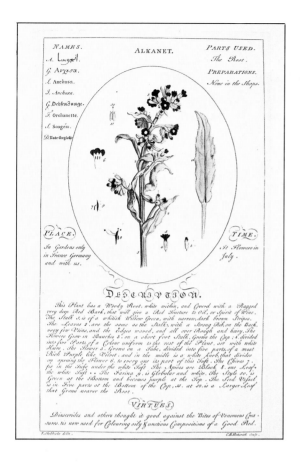

been undertaken previously and has not been equalled since. Reissues in 1976 in paperback (with a cover design that confounds all but the botanists!), the work retains its popularity. The book was compiled over many years and behind it is a story of dedication and diligence on the part of the author but alas one of manipulation which eventually broke her health.

Soon after Mrs Leyel had founded the Society of Herbalists in 1927 she received a complete list of Maud Grieve's 1000 pamphlets, the result of more than fifteen years work, and, as she says in the Introduction to *A Modern Herbal* she 'thought they might be the nucleus of the much needed herbal'.

Hilda Leyel arranged to have the collection of leaflets published by Mr Jonathan Cape and she edited Maud Grieve's work in so far as presentation was concerned, but comparison of the leaflets with the published book reveals that only little information on American plants was appended or corrected. The author of the leaflets collaborated but from her papers it is clear that she was quite overshadowed by Mrs Leyel and was not even able to write a word of introduction to the book. Although Maud Grieve's work had been accepted by the most eminent pharmacists and botanists, her subsequent work was 'blocked' with the result that Maud Grieve's later book was published in America, an unusual event at that time. In all probability she was helped by Louisa King (Mrs Francis King) who was spoken of as 'the Gertrude Jekyll of America'. She was a writer and gardener and collaborated in books on both sides of the Atlantic; in fact at the time she was contributing to one of Miss Eleanour Sinclair Rohde's books. Maud Grieve did, however, present typewritten copies of an updated version of *A Modern Herbal* to 'the authorities,' namely The Royal Botanic Gardens, Kew. However, by then she was in her mid-seventies and the strain proving too much, she suffered a nervous breakdown. Today such misfortunes are treated with understanding, but in the 1930s victims were isolated and information swept under the carpet. She was in fact eventually cared for privately and her work has survived to be acclaimed.

Timothy Sheldrake's exquisite draughtsmanship was accompanied by informative caption writing. Each herb then recognized by the College of Physicians was portrayed together with botanical details and suggestions for its herbal use in Botanicum Medicinale *(1759).*

IV

PHYSIC GARDENS
(1650–1800)

EARLY PHYSIC GARDENS

The physic gardens John Gerard sought to establish, in addition to his own, are among the earliest recorded apart from monastic undertakings. As surgeon and herbalist to Queen Anne, consort to James I, he was granted the lease of a plot of land on which to garden, provided that he supplied her with herbs, flowers and fruit. It seems highly probable that this piece of land stretched from the river Thames across the Strand to the area now known as Covent Garden. Previously he had attempted to establish a physic gardens for the company of Barber-Surgeons of which he was eventually to become Master in 1607.

'Physic' conveyed science or study, and set such gardens apart from the newly evolving pleasure of decorative gardens. Such enterprises had been established already in Europe at Padua in Italy, for example, and at Palermo's medical schools, expressly for the study of physic or medicinal plants. So for some years following their incorporation, the apothecaries sought to establish their own garden if only to study some of the newly arrived plants from overseas.

It was James I who encouraged the incorporation of the apothecaries as a Guild, separating them from the Grocers' Company with whom they had been combined since 1378. The remark that grocers were merchants but the apothecary's trade was a mystery is attributed to James I (the word 'mystery' here used with its old connotation of art or craft.) By 1617 the Worshipful Company of Apothecaries of London was incorporated with 114 apothecaries 'being His Majesty's natural subjects' together with a few foreigners working in London, who became associates. Simultaneously it was enacted that no grocer should keep an apothecary's shop and that medicines were not to be sold by the barber-surgeons. Thus the apothecaries were given a rightful place as a respected professional body; their establishment could be searched and drugs examined in both London and the provinces. At that time botany and medicine had yet to take their individual courses of development; thus we find the physicians growing medicinal plants for instruction, the apothecaries and barber-surgeons, for use. The practice then was for the physician to diagnose and prescribe and for the apothecary to dispense and attend the patient, so the ability to identify plants accurately was part of professional integrity. In addition, since the late fourteenth century they had been largely responsible for certifying the wares of the drug merchants and herb gatherers.

CHELSEA PHYSIC GARDEN

A suitable plot of land of three acres, one rod and thirty five perches is first mentioned in the minutes of the Society of Apothecaries in June 1674 when it was resolved to build a wall around it. The plot had come into their possession the previous year leased from Charles Cheyne, afterwards Lord Cheyne, for £5 per annum, but recurring financial trouble had delayed any serious attempt towards making a garden. The site was ideal, on the north bank of the river Thames about three miles west of London and near the village of Chelsea. At the time the Society's funds were in a parlous state, as they were rebuilding their Hall, destroyed by the great city fire eight years previously; a fire in which some of them had lost their houses and shops also. Even in the early 1690s the garden could still not be described as flourishing and the Society considered abandoning it, although by that time the enclosing wall had been completed. In fact a plaque in the wall which proclaims *Hortus Botanicus Societatis Pharmaceuticae Lond.*

1686 commemorates a point in the development of the garden when it was considered to be adequately arranged and catalogued. Not only was the garden reasonably planted and a boathouse built near their water gate onto the river, but exchange visits had begun with physic gardens on the Continent. John Watts, one of the apothecaries who had contributed considerable sums of money towards the building of the wall, was sponsored by the Society to visit the botanic or physic garden at Leyden in Holland. However, in spite of an increasingly worthy botanical collection of plants and popular herborizing forays into the countryside for members and students, the shaky coffers tested the determination to carry on of new generations of apothecaries. Not until Sir Hans Sloane had purchased the Manor of Chelsea, including the apothecaries' garden in 1712 was their eventual benefactor to come on the scene. In fact a decade was to pass before their new landlord contrived the solution to their financial shortcomings, and in the long term preserved the garden for posterity.

As a young man Sir Hans Sloane had studied botany at the Physic Garden under John Watts, and after some years pursuing medicine in France, he practised in London. Then he travelled to Jamaica as physician to the Governor and married the wealthy widow of a Jamaican planter before returning to London where he later became President of the College of Physicians and President of the Royal Society. His solution to the instability of the Chelsea Physic Garden was to accept a yearly payment of £5, and to finance much of the maintenance and rebuilding; in return the apothecaries were to supply the Royal Society of London with 50 dried botanical specimens each year, of plants grown in the garden. The benefit to The Royal Society's collection is obvious, perhaps less so is the value of the record of plants known in the Garden during the eighteenth century.

By 1722 Sir Hans Sloane was instrumental in appointing Philip Miller to supervise the work of the Chelsea Physic Garden, an appointment that was to put the Garden on the international map in the botanical world. Nevertheless, Miller did not lose sight of the purpose of the garden, namely as a place for study of plants of value to man. By 1733 the apothecaries raised a marble statue by Rysbrack in the garden to Sir Hans Sloane, a replica of which stands at the centre today.

Philip Miller

As the century progressed Philip Miller's work while at the Chelsea Garden gained supreme importance in the three-pronged advance in the plant world of horticulture, botany and medicine. While the apothecaries had established the garden half a century before for the study of physic plants, they had set about assembling a wider range of plants, many of them new to these shores fully aware that the potential healing virtue had yet to be explored. Miller compiled a catalogue of medicinal plants by 1730, and by his travels and painstaking correspondence accumulated a knowledge of the plant world unchallenged in England at the time. His contributions to both the expanding science of botany and to the developing craft of horticulture were immeasurable and all credit is due to the Society of Apothecaries for supporting the work. Miller is popularly known as the author of *The Gardeners Dictionary* (and its many editions and translations) and for numerous other writings on gardening. He describes in that major publication the familiar cultivated herbs but notes that 'what is missing is any real dissertation on herb gardens'. So while we may search in vain for descriptive accounts, there is affirmation that some existed. He provided the authority and the impetus, based on the Chelsea Physic Garden for international exchange of plants and research and later for embracing and elucidating the newly adopted binominal system of plant names propounded by Carl Linnaeus, the Swedish botanist. Miller truly held the reins of the three carriages of knowledge through an enormously exacting and quickly advancing period of expansion. Much of it went on within the walls of the apothecaries' physic garden.

OTHER PHYSIC GARDENS

While London and the London apothecaries were recovering from the Great Fire a small physic garden was established in 1670 in Edinburgh on a plot of land no more than 40 feet square at Holyrood Abbey. Very soon it was overstocked with medicinal plants and the collection was moved to land leased from Edinburgh Town Council to a

A watercolour of the Chelsea Physic Garden painted by J W Fuge c 1830, looking south west towards the river.

'An accurate survey of the Botanic Garden at Chelsea' . . . 'Survey'd and delineated' by John Haynes (1751). Shown clearly is the central statue of Sir Hans Sloane, the four cedar trees, the apothecaries' barge house and the water gate on to the River Thames.

site alongside Trinity Hospital, now part of Waverley Station. By the mid-1690s, a third site was brought into cultivation as part of the Royal Garden at Holyrood known as the King's Garden; the two latter became rival schools of botany. Only for about forty years did such twin channels of learning survive and then by the appointment of one man, Charles Alston, to supervise both gardens, a lasting merger was effected. The appointment held the joint honour of University Chair and King's Botanist, a custom perpetuated until 1956.

Meanwhile at Oxford the garden started in 1621 had survived through a sequestered period during the Civil Wars (see page 45). By 1670 King Charles II put in his own physician, a Scot named Robert Morrison who lectured out of doors regularly on herbs and other plants in the garden, with a table before him for his plant specimens. Morrison was the first Professor of Botany at Oxford (he died in 1683 as a result of having been knocked down by a carriage in Trafalgar Square, London). Just as the curios and abnormal plant forms had intrigued Gerard and Parkinson and their contemporaries, diversity of pigment attracted Morrison's attention. He initiated a collection of variegated-leaved plants, a feature for which the garden remains renowned today. The latter half of the seventeenth century was a period during which the study of botany developed, and it was as an aspect of botanical investigation that Morrison devoted himself to that work.

THE ADVANCE OF BOTANY

Great advances were afoot in the scientific investigation of plants spurred on by the increasing use of the microscope. Up to that time botany had been little more than the handmaid of medicine and the apothecaries, or herbalists as they were soon to be considered, probably knew their plants better than most. They had for the past 500 years classified the plant kingdom into trees, shrubs and herbs with no regard to relationships or similarities of plants. John Parkinson had sorted them out in a simple way, but John Ray, son of a blacksmith, is credited with propelling botany forward in

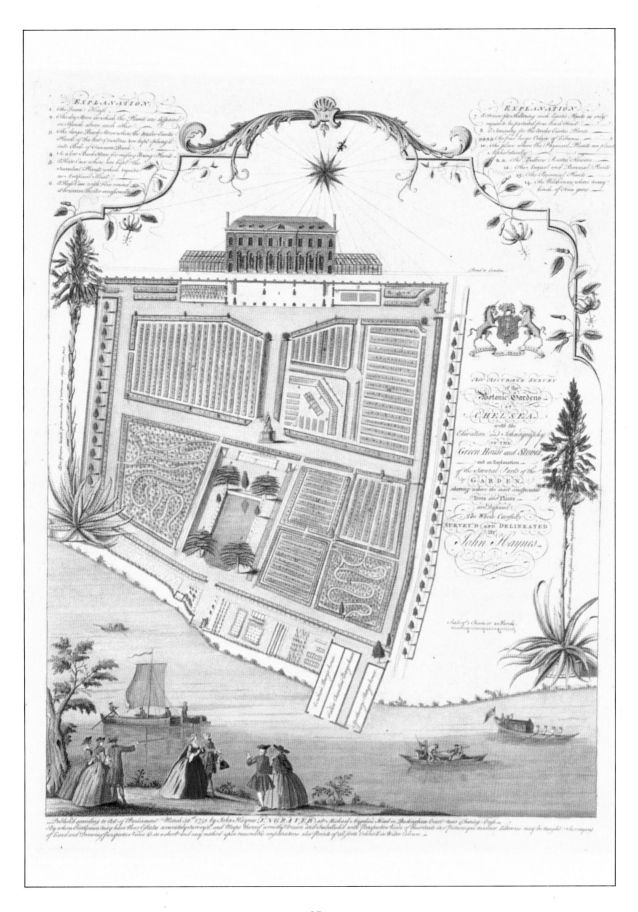

England, for it had lagged behind Continental ideas. He endeavoured to 'herborize' as Thomas Johnson had done some thirty years earlier, and made extensive tours over much of Britain studying local plants, many of which were herbs. His study led him to a far more scholarly assessment of the classification of plants and his salient contribution to botany was *Historia Plantarum Generalis* (1686–1704). In England at least, this proved the way for the acceptance of the theories of the binominal system of Carl Linnaeus in the following century. Before then various attempts were made to classify plants. Dr William Withering, who is credited with discovering the value of the foxglove to provide the principle digitalis, published *Arrangement of British Plants* (1776 and later editions), based upon a stamen counting system for classification.

This was the period in which the common botanical terms were formulated which we learn at school today. Robert Hooke, botanist, physicist and chemist, investigated cork through the lens of his microscope and named the perforations 'cells'. Nehemiah Grew, a Coventry man who studied at Cambridge and Leyden and practised as a doctor and botanist in Coventry and London, coined the term 'radicle' for a young root, and 'plume' for the embryonic stem, now known as the plumule. It was John Ray who first commited to paper the word 'petal' in 1682. Prior to that period *pot pourri* had been formed of 'rose leaves'. So as the science of botany forged ahead to investigate the wonders of the structure of the plant world, and the gardeners marvelled at new and exotic treasures from across the seas, it was left to the housewives and common people to continue to grow herbs as economic favourites in their gardens, and to the herbalists (apothecaries) to deal in them. Fewer authoritative herbals were published and herbs were included in the general writings about what today would be considered kitchen gardens, or they were regarded as drug plants and their medicinal properties described in the developing pharmacopoeia.

The formal layout of the Oxford Physic Garden as it was known when it was laid out in 1621, has been maintained. The Danby Gate (inset l and R) was then the height of modernity, and it remains the main entrance.

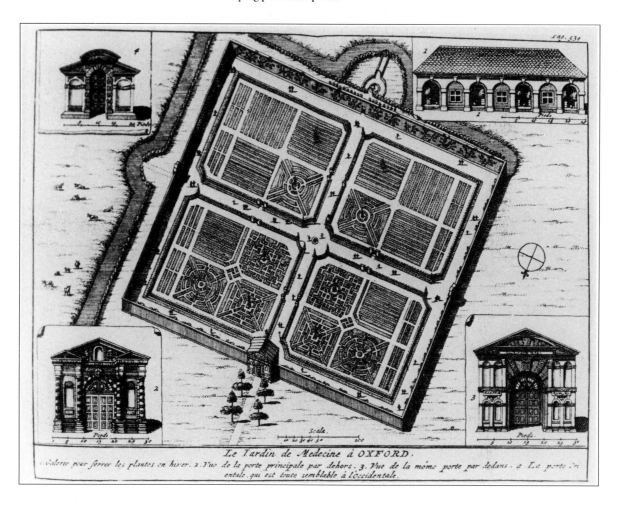

Le Tardin de Medecine à OXFORD.

NICHOLAS CULPEPER

One important herbal of this period, which makes an equal claim to fame today alongside Gerard's work was *The English Physician* compiled by Nicholas Culpeper (see page 55). A couple of centuries had gone by since William Turner had prepared the first herbal for the common people, writing about their own plants and in their own language. Culpeper's motives were stronger: he attempted to expose the mysteries of the herb trade and the exclusive knowledge of the apothecaries and doctors so that the artisans, merchants, travellers and housewives could extend their own repertoire of remedies and heal themselves because they were unable to face the high fees demanded by the professional practitioners. He roused the fury of physicians by his translation into English (from the learned Latin) of the *London Pharmacopoeia* — their 'Secret Handbook' — but, undaunted, Culpeper chose independence of thought.

What Culpeper remains notorious for is his adherence to the astrological botany and to the Doctrine of Signatures. Astrological botany had had its disciples since the Ancient World (and continues to do so), but at that time the Doctrine of Signatures was something of a retrograde step dipping back into Medieval beliefs. Nicholas Culpeper revived the theory, and in bringing it to the surface in the seventeenth century, has probably ensured our popular knowledge of the subject.

The Doctrine of Signatures

Throughout the Middle Ages, a rule whereby it was believed that plants displayed their intended use, had its adherents. It was in the intepretation of such signs that the understanding of healing plants rested. Parts of the plant were believed to represent that part of the body, or the condition for which they were intended. The felted leaves of the coltsfoot and mullein were suggestive of mucus and thus indicated their use in the treatment of coughs. The eyebright displayed markings and shape that indicated its intended use for treatment of the eyes and the form of the walnut (*Juglans regia*) was likened to the brain and therefore recommended for headaches and madness. For similar reasons of form, the tiny tubers of the lesser celandine were meant to relieve haemorrhoids and earned the name pilewort for the plant. It became a persuasive doctrine that not only designated uses but gave vernacular names to many herbs. *Pulmonaria* or lungwort with its lung-shaped leaves and spittle-like splashes took both its scientific and common names in support of the theory. Colour appears to have played a role: red roses cured nose bleeding, geranium stemmed haemorrhage and yellow juices of saffron and turmeric, jaundice of the liver and biliousness. The long calyx of the campanula indicated sore throats, the down on a quince meant it prevented hair from falling and the henbane seed receptacle resembled the jaw, suggesting toothache and gum disorders.

Sometimes the sign was more obscure and might represent an animal, the bite of which was to be treated by the plant; the adder's tongue (*Ophioglossum vulgatum*) for instance was to be applied to the bite of the adder. At its limit, the belief demanded that some plants were purposely left blank in order to encourage investigation of their healing properties. In the ambiguity over symbolism and the natural therapeutic value of the plant lay the weakness of the whole theory. However, it fired man's awareness of botanical intricacies in a period when such interests were being extended. In itself the Doctrine of Similarities or Signatures, where 'like treats like' was to prove a blind alley in the progress of medical knowledge, although the idea was supported in the later theories of homoeopathy.

Culpeper's theories seem incredibly obtuse today and he was in fact dabbling in a form of astrological botany, which in common with many other subjects becomes debased by popular or universal use. His confused reasoning, incorporating the planets under which herbs grew, relating these to the ruling planet of the disease to be treated, and simultaneously having regard to the form of the plant significant for its use, creates a maze of misconceptions. However, the seventeenth-century mind with its scientific and mathematical predilections seems to have swallowed Culpeper's ideas unquestioningly. Surprisingly he was convinced totally himself, that he alone had a clarity of understanding that surpassed all previous writers of herbals. In his preface he says that former writers were 'as full of nonsense and contradictions as an Egg is full of meat'.

While William Coles 'upheld' the theory of the Doctrine of Signatures, he refuted totally Culpeper's interpretations of astrological botany. His reason for doing so was that the Sun, Moon and Stars were created on the fourth day whereas the plants were made on the third. As far as Coles was concerned, that was the end of the matter.

The Doctrine he explained as 'Through Sin and Satan have plunged mankinde into an Ocean of Infirmities Yet the mercy of God which is over all his Workes Maketh Grasse to grow upon the Mountaines and Herbs for the use of Men and hath not onely stemped upon them (as upon every man) a distinct forme, but also given them particular signatures, whereby Man may read even in legible Characters and Use them'.

Astrological botany

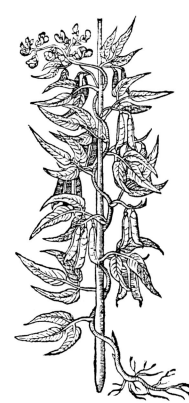

We have seen that the allocation of plants to the gods of the Ancient World led to some plants being ruled by planets once the names were transferred from gods to planets. Culpeper as an exponent of seventeenth-century astrological influences upon plant life placed herbs under the dominion of the sun, moon or one of the (then) five known planets and enumerated in his *Astrological Judgment of Diseases* the parts of the body governed by the same planets and signs of the Zodiac. The theory was ancient, but it was Culpeper who pushed the belief and made its structure generally available to the common people. Even today the astrological theories of vegetation are sound, as being affected by the phases of the moon, the increase in growth or proliferation of cells is most marked towards the new moon. Throughout the 13 lunar phases through the seasons the acceleration of growth in plants is most obvious prior to a full moon, and by the influence of the season, more marked (in the northern hemisphere) before the full moons of April and May than that of December and January.

Simultaneously, astrological botany was confounded with the hieroglyphics of the 'signature' of the plant. Such tenuous connections almost smacked of old-fashioned ritualistic belief when, for example, it was said that the root of plantains was good for headaches because 'the signe of the Ramme (Aries) is supposed to be the house of the planete Mars, which is the head of the whole worlde'. Stress was laid upon the hour at which a herb should be gathered or even the planetary transit or conjunction that was most effective. Somehow we cannot help thinking that many of these ideas were little more than a pseudoscientific overlay of well-worn traditions harking back to the rituals and folklore of the Dark and Middle Ages.

TO THE NEW WORLD

The herbals of Gerard, in its Johnson-revised form, of Parkinson and of Culpeper, were important travelling companions and indispensable aids for the increasing number of English who were setting out for the New World. They sent for many seeds; some plants they found there were almost identical to some they knew, many were unfamiliar. The Puritans took very few plants that were considered to have occult connections, and those plants they did import were to influence their way of life and of course, their gardens. During the years of establishment in North America the 'practitioners of Physick' were invariably clergymen, just as in Medieval Europe the professions of clergy and doctor had been closely linked. Thus they treated both men's souls and bodies and relied upon the book of Genesis and other biblical passages that assured them that herbs were on the earth for man's benefit. Their limited understanding accepted a 'kill or cure' hypothesis. If the patient recovered, the correct balance had been restored to his system; if not, then it was God's will that had to be accepted. Disease simply regarded as dis-ease or imbalance was some alien visitor to the body that had to be dealt with. The wider thinking of the 'whole person' today had a relevance even though the existence of the immune system was then unknown.

New England gardens

Many a homesick wife made a plot of herbs, not only to support her family but to remind her of home, and she included many English flowers and herbs. We have scant impressions of the early gardens of New England but can form a fair picture from the reports of an Englishman who visited America. John Josselyn must have been of an enquiring nature and wrote *New England's Rarities Discovered* (1672) which remains as a lasting record of what he found thriving there, and indeed of his uninhibited enthusiasm for it all. Among the herbs he saw dill, coriander, hollyhock (mallow), ground ivy, pennyroyal, lavender cotton, spearmint, rue ('will hardly grow'), feverfew, smallage, elecampane, comfrey, anise, sorrel, celandine ('grows but slowly') tansy and dittany. Those plants that struggled through the bitter winters, or which did not thrive he listed as lavender, rosemary, bay, clary, southernwood and fennel 'must be taken up, and kept in a Cellar all Winter'.

Josselyn's background interest in plants allowed him to categorize plants he found there under headings: 'Such plants as are common with us in England: Such plants as are proper to the Country, Such plants as are proper to the country and have no name, Such plants as have sprung up since the English planted and kept cattle in New England'. (He was writing half a century after the arrival of the first settlers.) Many English 'weeds' are credited with crossing the Atlantic at that time, possibly as seed in ballast, packing, sacking and of course some as seed to sow. He suggested these English 'weeds' to be nettle, plantain, henbane, motherwort, groundsel, mullein, wild mustard and wormwood.

ERYNGO

Apart from minor crops grown in selected areas such as saffron at Saffron Walden, Essex, personal enterprise sometimes prevailed. Colchester in Essex became known in the seventeenth century for candied eryngo root or kissing comfits. Gerard gave the recipe of 'the manner to condite Eringos' explaining a soaking and boiling process, 'then must they be pilled clean as ye pil parsneps and the pith must be drawn out at the end of the root'. A candying process followed, boiling in sugar and orange flower water and the strips were then dried. Gerard recommended 'have in readinesse great cap or royall papers, whereupon you straw some sugar, upon which lay your roots having taken them out of the pan. These papers you must put into a stouve or hot-house to harden; but if you have not such a place, lay them before a good fire: in this manner you condite your roots'. The process used over a couple of centuries in Colchester appears to have been the same. Roots were cut into strips and twisted like barley sugar sticks before the candying process.

Robert Buxton, an apothecary of Colchester, introduced such sweetmeats into general use about 1620, and following his fall from favour after the Civil War, the trade was continued by his apprentice Samuel Great (of Dutch extraction, formerly de Groot), the trade being retained by his family certainly until 1797 although considerable quantities were sold well into the nineteenth century both at home and for foreign consumption.

It was customary to present eminent visitors to the town with eryngo root sweetmeats for which attractive oval wooden boxes were made; one such presentation was made to Queen Charlotte as she passed through the town following her arrival in England. Roots were unearthed from the sandy beaches of Clacton, Dovercourt and Mersea, and proved a tough assignment as the best portions were about 1.8 m (6 ft) below the surface.

THE GENTLE ART OF GARDENING

While botanists and herbalists mulled over their varied theories, expanding opportunities for travel fostered the advance in gardening practice and ideas. Plant collections were established and built up for newly-introduced genera and species faster than ever before. Between the first and eighth editions of Philip Miller's *The Gardeners Dictionary* the number of plants recorded at the Chelsea Physic Garden increased by about 4000. They came from the New World, West Indies, Eastern and Northern Europe, Siberia and The Cape. The horticultural nursery trade expanded simultaneously and the art and craft of gardening, or cultivation and propagation, developed in every way, infiltrating the philosophy and culture of the English. Vast new estates were laid out in the fashionable style that emulated the rolling meadow and copse landscape,

while the new flowering plants, as well as newly tried vegetables were confined behind newly established kitchen garden walls.

Town and small gardens were as little recorded as are housing estate gardens today. Sketchy evidence suggests that some gardeners augmented their living by distilling lavender or peppermint, sometimes both, as did a Mr Baker of Crossbankdale in Derbyshire, who in 1812 was reported to have formerly cultivated 'on a good scale'. Sale bills for mint distilling equipment, and valuations of crops of peppermint, or of a mint yard, emerge from time to time when examining archives. Herb or physic plant growers obviously worked on a small scale quite unworthy of written records. In the will of George Singleton (1735) of the Parish of St Georges, Hanover Square, London, he is described as a 'Physick Gardener'. It is self-evident, however, that household culinary, scented and physic plants continued to be grown in little plots but were no longer treasures to be written about and illustrated. The eighteenth century brought a spate of amazingly beautiful flower books or florigea depicting new-found wonders exquisitely portrayed by the quickly advancing craft of the printer.

Distilling and Other Physical Herbs

For the new vast kitchen gardens, Batty Langley set down the rules in *New Principles* (1728) and offered a 'Design for an elegant kitchen garden after a new and grand manner' and another 'environed with Espaliers of Fruit'. His list of distilling and other physical herbs 'as are absolutely necessary for the Services of all Gentlemen (and other) families in general' is commentary upon the amounts of herbs required and emphasizes their importance in the early part of the century before many vegetables known today were introduced.

Balm, bugloss, burrage, burnet, marigold and savory had each a rod (3 metres), chamomile 4 rods; other beds were to include cardus, clary, comfrey, dragon and dill, a rod of each and 10 rods of clove gillyflower. A third bed was to hold dwarf elder, hyssop, elecampane, fennel and feverfew, 2 rods of each, a rod of spike lavender, 2 of common lavender, 2 of lavender cotton and 6 rods of marigolds. So the list goes on setting out the garden in true potager fashion with 'licorish', mint, violets, tansy, angelica, roses, rosemary, sage, marsh mallow, saffron, Solomon's seal, wormwood, scurvy grass, pennyroyal, tobacco and rue, and in addition as many beds devoted to 'Kitchen Herbs, Roots, Pulse, etc'.

WILLIAM CURTIS (1747–1799)

The name William Curtis first appears in 1773 when he was appointed 'Praefactus horti and Demonstrator of plants' to the Society of Apothecaries at their physic garden in Chelsea. Born at Alton, Hampshire (where there is now a museum to his memory) into a Quaker family he was first apprenticed to his grandfather, a surgeon-apothecary, and later to London apothecaries and attended lectures at St Thomas's Hospital although his overriding interest was in natural history, one he shared with many friends. When he was 25 years of age he sold his apothecary's practice to his partner and turned his attention to writing about plants and the development of his garden near Grange Road, Bermondsey, where he proposed to cultivate British native plants rather than the curio-like exotics which were the rage of the horticultural world. *Flora Londinensis* the first volume of which appeared between 1775 and 1781, during which period William Curtis resigned his office as Demonstrator of Plants at the Chelsea Physic Garden to devote himself to various literary activities and to laying out what was to become The London Botanic Garden at Lambeth Marsh. The approximate site is that of the Festival of Britain Exhibition (1951). Curtis described the plot as 'peculiarly favourable to the growth of aquatic and bog plants, and all such as love a moist bottom'. By 1783 Curtis published *A Catalogue of the British Medicines, Culinary and Agricultural plants cultivated in the London Botanic Garden*. This catalogue also included a list of books in the botanic garden library, and the privileges afforded to members or subscribes for receiving plants and seeds, and for walking in the garden. Donations of plant material came from Kew, from the Chelsea Physic Garden and from private gardens such as those belonging to Dr Fothergill at Upton, Essex; The Duchess of Portland at Bulstrode,

Bucks; The Rev. John Lightfoot her botanist; Sir Joseph Banks and several nurserymen.

Curtis is, of course, best remembered for launching a sumptuous publication *The Botanical Magazine* universally referred to as the 'Bot Mag' and which has proved to be the oldest scientific periodical of its kind in the world with richly coloured plates. However the relevance of Curtis's work here is as a none-too-dedicated apothecary and the instigator of a private botanic garden in which native plants, and above all native medicinal and culinary herbs had their rightful place. Contemporary writers were indulging in garden design, arboriculture, introduced plants and the development of horticultural practice.

In 1786 Curtis embarked upon instalments of *Assistant plates to the materia medica; or figures of such plants and animals as are used in Medicine.* His purpose was to identify clearly the plants widely described in recent herbals, and to instruct medical students. While the publication was not long lived, it serves to indicate that there were, as Curtis pointed out 'medical gentlemen most intimately conversant with the effects of herbs, with whose exterior form they are totally unaquainted'.

William Curtis had been aware of the need for accurate engravings of official plants when he published *Assistant plates*, and failed to acknowledge the artist, although it is generally assumed to have been Sowerby. When Woodville compiled his *Medical Botany*, published between 1790 and 1795, it was James Sowerby whose draughtsmanship added so much to the value and usefulness of the folios. Dr William Woodville was a Quaker physician from Cumbria, who settled in London and made a botanic garden in the precincts of the Smallpox Hospital, St Pancras. In the preface he states: 'It is justly a matter of surprise, that notwithstanding the universal adoption of the Linnaean system of botany, and the great advances made in natural science, the works of Blackwell and Sheldrake should still be the only books in the country in which copper-plate figures of the medicinal plants are professedly given'. All the plants in the *materia medica* catalogues of the Royal College of Physicians of London and Edinburgh are illustrated, and today provide historical reference not only for the treatment of the sick but for the numerous plants cultivated in those physic gardens. *Medical Botany* continued to be published and remained a standard work for the ensuing 80 years.

The eighteenth century endowed a seemingly moribund atmosphere on physic gardens proper. Almost as if some enclosed plot were hanging on to the past while the gardeners, without any sense of nostalgia, had fled. They had fled to grow the exciting, newly acquired overseas plants, bigger and brighter and often more highly scented. Academic physic gardens were transformed into botanic gardens and the academic interest in herbalism plunged to its lowest ebb. In rural districts folk cures remained popular, but the cultivating of economic herbs became a horticultural backwater, and herbs and herb gardens almost ceased to be written about or recorded.

Plant riches from all parts of the explored world were collected in the Chelsea Physic Garden by Philip Miller. No doubt the apothecaries displayed a keen interest in them as this Victorian vignette suggests. It represents a discussion group of apothecaries in 1750.

V

INDUSTRIAL MIST
(1800–1915)

HUMBLE ROLES FOR HERBS

Botanical exploration by both amateur and professional botanists in their own fields developed with zealous activity as the nineteenth century began. Thanks to the recently propounded Linnaean system of classifying plants newly discovered species could be catalogued and their descriptions understood in a universal way. As the century advanced a curiosity about evolution developed with attendant questions regarding plant relationships, which resulted in huge herbaria being amassed. Notably, these belonged to universities and botanic gardens; some remain relevant to today's research, others have been dispersed. Botanical excitements have centred on exotic plants, and the native herbs have been overlooked, but today many plants are being reassessed as we shall see.

The herbs, especially the native and naturalized species were considered to be old fashioned early in the nineteenth century by the rising educated classes, and exotic herbs and mineral drugs occupied the attention of the medical profession. Herbs remained the remedies to be relied upon, both medical and household, for the country people and the mid-century poor who inhabited the towns that sprang up around the brute labour forces of developing industries. Such urban communities proved breeding grounds for herbal vendors and charlatans. A fantastic amount of ineffective rubbish must have been sold.

Rural communities still gathered their own herbs from the meadows and hedgerows and as the century advanced towards a near fatal agricultural depression the country-side had to provide not only the medicines, but the conserves, beverages, the insect repellents and the festival flowers. Old customs remained; folklore surrounded every occasion; country names for herbs and all other wild plants disregarded the high and mighty scientific appellations and as the amateur botanists and 'wild flower enthusiasts' trooped into the countryside to search for plants to paint, to record or to press for their personal herbaria, the folklore trailed from Medieval minds into Victorian parlours. The language of flowers was revived and newly sentimentalized, wild flower books appeared endowing each plant with a dozen 'local' names and eulogizing upon its 'old-fashioned' qualities and fairy lore.

Tisanes

Old-fashioned ideas led to the fetish of drinking tisanes or herb teas, not so much as a therapeutic beverage, but as a folk cure or 'grandmother's' recipe. Country wines enjoyed popularity: dandelion and burdock, elderberry, elderflower and cowslip; country remedies remained Victorian favourites: marigold cream for sunburn, poppy heads for sprains, knitbone for torn ligaments, chamomile for hair rinses, licorice for tummy upsets, peppermint for flatulence and indigestion and feverfew for headaches. As 'grandmother's' tisanes, they enjoyed a revival in Victorian drawing rooms and conservatories. Golden yellow chamomile tea was sweetish, almost sickly; lemon balm producing a cooling green tea; pale yellow elderflower tea with a fruity flavour resembled that made from meadowsweet. Sage tea was a favourite sometimes combined with betony as a home remedy to reduce fevers and allay nervous disorders, saffron tea had a reputation for combatting measles and vervain, hop, chamomile, nettle

Victorian ladies delighted in pot pourri. Geoge Dunlop Leslie's painting portrays the making of pot pourri with rose petals, dried lavender flowers and spices from the caster.

and comfrey root, sometimes combined, helped to induce sleep. Primrose tea relieved gout and rheumatism, thyme tea or catnep tea calmed digestive dispepsia.

Soft drinks or 'lemonades' often combining two or three herbs were popularly made, perhaps using lemon balm with woodsorrel, wild marjoram with rose hips or wild strawberries; cough candy included horehound and coltsfoot. Vinegars were flavoured with dill, tarragon, rosemary and lavender and relishes made containing caraway and fennel seed, angelica, rhubarb and sage. All this was enchantingly old-world, a tradition from earlier generations and gradually became overshadowed by the manufactured and synthetic 'potent' tonics and medicines, the highly flavoured condiments of Victorian culinary arts along with the readily available quack remedies on every market and from every itinerant salesman.

Calomel, opium, laudanum and other lethal drugs were freely available and smart medicine chests were the order of the domestic day for the town housewife. No longer was she expected to reign over a productive stillroom, but she had a lavish medicine chest of polished wood, complete with brass locks and innumerable bottles of cut glass set in velvet sockets all accompanied by a detailed 'medical guide'. The humble herbs had been well and truly relegated.

Victorian pot pourri

Sweet bags and scented sachets, often trimmed with lace, threaded with ribbon or embroidered with an affectionate message were favourite personal gifts among Georgian and Victorian ladies. Richly fragrant moist pot pourri had reached its zenith of popularity in the late eighteenth century and became increasingly complex during the Georgian period. By the mid-nineteenth century the lazier free-for-all dry pot pourri was made by impecunious country dwellers and sold in the town markets and fairs at considerable profit. Whichever combinations were preferred, beautiful pot pourri bowls, open or perforated, were made of porcelain or pottery; silver or wooden boxes with fretted lid were pressed into use and filled to scent closets, parlours and bedrooms.

Miss Jekyll described her method of making pot pourri towards the end of the century, as if it represented some harvest home celebration. Bushels of rose petals and scented geranium leaves were dried and pressed a layer at a time into large jars, which she had had made specially for the purpose, sprinkled with bay salt and held down by lead weights. Later further dried petals and salt were added, a layer at a time and held down. Separate jars held various ingredients through the summer months. Then at the end of October came a great 'Pot Pourri Party', with tea to follow!

'A space is swept on the brick floor . . . the full jars are brought into a wide circle, one mixer is posted at each bowl and the materials are thrown handful by handful on the floor in the middle space, after each pressed layer has been broken up by a fork or prong.' She describes how the 'posts of honour' go to the distributors of orange peel pierced with cloves, and the 'sauce' composed of five large packets of Atkinson's Violet Powder, 1 lb each of allspice, cloves, mixed spice, mace, gum benzoin, gum storax together with powdered mace and powdered cloves. The 'head pot pourri maker' then began to turn the heap with a shovel, backwards and forwards, left to right and then it was all rammed into an oak cask of 15 gal (68.25 l) capacity, pressed down and locked in. There it remained for 'some weeks or even months'. Small wonder that the *ad hoc* dry pot pourri-making gained popularity among twentieth-century housewives.

COMMERCIAL HERB GROWING

Licorice

The general assumption is that licorice (*Glycyrrhiza glabra*) was introduced into England by the Black Friars: John of Gaddesden writing in fourteenth-century Oxford suggested a lengthy list of remedies against scrofulous glands, adding that if all else failed an application of 'snails and licorice' should be made. William Turner mentioned it in 1548 and the apothecaries knew one form in their physic gardens (*G. vulgaris*). Confirmation of its cultivation on a commercial scale in the eighteenth century comes from John Perfect of Pontefract, Yorkshire, a subscriber to both Stephen Switzer's *The*

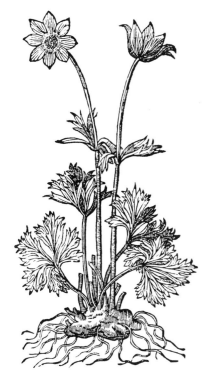

In Georgian and early Victorian households many preserves, cosmetics and medicines were prepared from herbs. Here flowers are drying and preserves being stored in a still room.

Practical Husbandman and Planter and to Philip Miller's *The Gardeners Dictionary*. The making of 'Spanish' or Spanish licorice was in full progress in the town of Pontefract during the eighteenth century, the boiled licorice root being pressed into little 'Licorice Cakes' and stamped with a pattern resembling the ancient castle of the town; these were sold in green and black enamelled tins. They remained the speciality of the town throughout the nineteenth century and were readily available until the middle of this century. The licorice fields of Pontefract remained, resembling areas of young ash plants, and have diminished gradually under economic pressures.

Lesser commercial crops

Of the lesser herb crops, chamomile was grown in Surrey and in Derbyshire, coriander and saffron in Essex, all for the confectioners', distillers' and druggists' trades. A region noted for rhubarb growing was around Wakefield, Yorkshire, where it was destined for

*Drying teazels (*Dipsacus fullonum*) at Fivehead, Somerset during the 1960s.*

the local markets rather than the druggists' trade. There, family concerns grew individual varieties, guarding their stock with considerable pride, but official rhubarb was cultivated on the borders of Oxfordshire and Northamptonshire by William Rufus Usher who concentrated on *Rheum rhaponticum* as well as *Rheum officinalis*; he was widely known as a grower from about 1841. Mr Usher's rhubarb farm was described by Bentley and Trimmer in *Medicinal Plants* (1880) as 'the only place in England where it is cultivated for its roots and the annual yield is about ten tons'. The roots were sliced and dried for the druggists and sold as 'fine large flats' and 'fine large rounds'.

Spearmint was a market crop raised around Fulham in London and on dampish ground near Isleworth and Gunnersbury south of the Thames. Mr Elliot, a market gardener of Fulham, had several long ranges of heated pits in the 1880s in which to force mint from autumn to spring. Various mints were grown for distilling on smallholdings in different parts of England whose siting was dependent upon accessibility to a local still. The practice of growing mint for distillation appears in eighteenth-century records when proven wills reveal mint stills as an effect, sometimes even existing stocks of oil of peppermint. In the nineteenth century, the practice of using small local stills died out and larger commercial stills dealt with bulkier crops. As many as ten weeks' distilling was carried on night and day in some of them. Hitchin in Hertfordshire, Long Melford and Market Deeping in Lincolnshire and Mitcham in Surrey, are generally listed as the main commercial mint growing areas in England.

Gradually the economic tide began to swamp the minor commercial enterprises. Wholesale drug companies organized their own farms and the bulk of vegetable drugs was imported into the United Kingdom. One of the last physic gardens in London to distil its own medical preparations was that of the Clock House in Chelsea, owned by a

Miss Howard as late as 1828. Her distilled waters were held in high esteem among wealthy and distinguished households. Physic gardens existed elsewhere through the nineteenth century and some into the early twentieth. Crop reports, for example for 1913, show cultivation being carried on by Ransoms at Hitchin, Potter and Clarke (formerly Potter and Moore) at Mitcham, Mr Seymour at Holbeach, Norfolk, and Mr Bing at Grove Ferry, Kent.

Culinary herbs

The decline in smallholdings for the cultivation of medicinal plants was compensated by an increasing market for parsley, sage and watercress. Parsley and sage began to be grown as minor crops near many local brisk markets and watercress flourished in 'unpolluted' water beds mainly in chalk-drained areas. Cultivation began in the Lea Valley of Hertfordshire about 1860. In Hampshire, the oldest established watercress farms are around Andwell and Maplederwell near the sources of the river Loddon. Later, cultivation was established near Basing and Petersfield and around the sources of the river Rother at Steep and in the valleys of the Test and Itchen.

Teazels

The fullers teazel (*Dipsacus fullonum*) even in Gerard's day was listed as the 'garden teasell, or the tame teasell sown in this country in gardens to serve Fullers and Clothworkers'. The bracts of the wild plant are too soft and flexible to serve for combing in the cloth trade. Evidence exists of the cultivation of the teazel during the reign of Edward III and indeed into the present century in Somerset. Previously it was cropped in some northern cloth manufacturing areas and Essex, Wiltshire and Gloucestershire. Writing in the mid-nineteenth century, Anne Pratt says that teazel is planted 'that their chaffy heads may be used in carding wool. No mechanical contrivance answers this purpose so well as to supersede this primitive method of dressing woollen cloth'. Considerable care was necessary in drying the mature heads to avoid breaking the hooks. Large heads were termed 'Kings' and smaller ones 'Princes', the latter better suited to the finer fabrics. Wood broom, card teazel or gipsy's combs are well-recorded country names and Dyer in his poem *The Fleece* says 'Soon the clothier's shears And burler's thistle skims the surface sheen'.

As a herb, and then called Venus's bath for the considerable quantity of water retained by the stem-clasping large leaves, it was recommended for sore eyes and called '*virga pastoris*' in Chaucer's time. Henry Lyte wrote of it 'It is termed *Labrum Veneris* or *Laver Lavacrum* of the forme of the leaves, made up in fashion of a bason, which is never without water'.

PART OF THE LAVENDER STORY
Potter and Moore

It is accepted generally that the cultivation of physic plants as a commercial venture began in the Mitcham area of Surrey to the south-west of London about 1768 or 1769. These dates may be a little late because Ephraim Potter, the first of the family to style himself a 'physic gardener', died in 1775 and was succeeded by his son James and daughter Anne. She it was who married Benjamin Moore, a calico printer of Mitcham, and their eldest son, another James, was taken as a partner by his uncle, bringing into being the familiar name Potter and Moore so closely associated with lavender products throughout the nineteenth and early twentieth centuries. By that time James Potter was described as a botanical herbalist 'whose Botanical gardens are very extensive and who has works here for extracting the essence of all his botanical herbs'. He bequeathed the garden and attendant equipment to his nephew James Moore in 1799 when the area under herb cultivation was 250 acres (101.175 hectares) in the parishes of Mitcham, Merton and Carshalton in Surrey.

The five principal growers of lavender in the Mitcham area had 14 stills among them. Some distilleries flourished for two centuries, emitting the rough smell of unrefined lavender oil over the Surrey villages. Peppermint too was distilled there on a considerable scale, perhaps notably by the Miller family who acquired some of Potter and Moore's stills and other equipment when they controlled 1200 acres (489 hectares) of herbs, market gardening and orchards and paid out as much as £10 000 a year in wages.

Another name closely associated with the lavender farms of Surrey is that of Sprules. William Sprules' enterprise flourished in the mid-nineteenth century; he farmed 50 acres (20.235 hectares) and had two stills when he was in his thirties. He continued to expand and moved to Wallington about 1864 when physic plant farming enjoyed its heyday. During the decline later in the century Sarah, his spinster daughter, navigated the enterprise through indifferent harvests and the threat of rural development, and maintained a distillery for lavender until her death in 1912. Her true delight was the special appointment 'Purveyors of Lavender Essence to the Queen' and the fact that she had strolled with Queen Victoria through the fields of lavender. The Queen is known to have been especially fond of lavender products.

Some growers in the district with small acreages under cultivation sent their harvests direct to Covent Garden; others such as Sprules or Newman had only one or two stills, whereas Potter and Moore by the mid-nineteenth century ran five large ones. Distillation costs increased as the century advanced and by the 1870s, the cost of the production of lavender oil in some instances was exceeding the market price. Something in the region of a pound to a pound and a half of oil resulted from a day's distilling, using 50 gal (227.5 l) of water to every 24 dozen bundles of lavender, each dozen bundles weighing about 20 lb (9.6 kg). Larger stills, such as those supervised at the Potter and Moore establishment (by mid-century owned by James Bridger, an illegitimate son of James Moore), had a capacity from 700–1000 gal (3195–4550 l) of water. Lavender was cut and bundled with stalks and called a mot, each of which weighed a hundred weight: 20 to 24 of these would fill a 1000 gall (4550 l) still.

Fifty years later, the principal crops cultivated commercially in the area were lavender, peppermint, and chamomile, and lesser crops included aconite, caraway, elecampane, licorice, foxglove, lovage, angelica, belladonna, squirting cucumber, poppy, rose, marsh mallow and savine (juniper). Surviving records indicate that three different mints, peppermint, spearmint and pennyroyal were among the first plants ever to be cultivated commercially in the Mitcham area, peppermint crops proving the most profitable, so that spearmint was planted only for forward orders. A ton of peppermint, yielded by simple contemporary stills, 2½–3 lb of oil.

Small domestic stills were familiar equipment in Georgian and Victorian households. This one had been used by William Ransom's grandmother to prepare remedies for her family.

William Ransom

Another prominent commercial grower of both lavender and peppermint was William Ransom, a Quaker of Hitchin in Hertfordshire. One of his school companions was Joseph Lister, later to distinguish himself as Lord Lister, the first surgeon to use an antiseptic treatment for wounds. William Ransom, having served a brief apprenticeship with Thomas and William Southall, manufacturing chemists of Birmingham, returned to his native town in 1845 and began cultivating medicinal plants (or vegetable drugs) for distillation by the time he was 20 years of age. A story was told that in old woolstapler's sheds belonging to his grandfather, which he was using, he found a small still which his grandmother had used for her household sweet herbs. A decade later he was known as a distiller of lavender and peppermint oils, and his farm quickly extended in various parts of Hitchin and Meppershall. Unlike the Mitcham growers he did not confine the manufactured products to home-grown plants, but imported herbs from all parts of the world and at the same time was an energetic botanist, archaeologist, magistrate, benefactor and successful manufacturing chemist. His life spanned the radical changes in the pharmaceutical industry which he navigated with certitude, and yet alongside he supported a rural industry which in season called upon women and children to collect wild flowers from the surrounding hedgerows. Gathering wild herbs for Mr Ransom was a seasonal occupation for we read of 'sunburnt and swarthy women and hordes of village children arriving with handcarts and wheelbarrows and aprons full of dandelion roots — as many as 12 tons of dandelions have been received at the Distillery in the course of a Saturday morning'. William Ransom started with about 70 acres (28.3 hectares) of land which by the middle of the present century extended to 250 acres (101 hectares), at least 200 (80) of which were devoted to medicinal plants. He died in his ninetieth year, and was succeeded by his only son Francis, a similarly capable pharmacist and business man. Together with a number of astute chemists and skilled personnel the family tradition is still carried on. In the story of herbs as *Materia Medica* a special place is allotted to Francis Ransom. Not only was he a highly respected

Lavender cultivated as a field crop being harvested on William Ransom's farm in Hitchin, Hertfordshire in the 1930s.

pharmacist who served on the Board of Examiners of the Pharmaceutical Society (as it was then), but a skilled researcher into some crude drugs which had been familiar to him from his boyhood. He is remembered for his work on belladonna in particular, which led to preparations of that drug being revolutionized, and for work on henbanes, ipecacuanha, nux vomica and digitalis. In 1885 he became his father's business partner and the name William Ransom and Son came into being. A wide range of herbs continued to be farmed for the on-the-spot preparation of galencial products. The Company continues to manufacture world-wide supplies of essential oils, tinctures, liniments, resins and chlorophyll.

Perks and Llewellyn

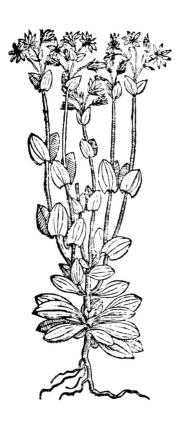

Another lavender-growing area, on the sunny slopes of a hill north of the town of Hitchin, probably belonged to James Meers round about 1780. Harry Perks was an apothecary-chemist established about 1760 and it seems to have been his son John who forged the lavender connection, by taking over Meers' Farm. In turn his son, Edward, began to specialize in lavender products at the beginning of the nineteenth century. Lavender toiletries from the Perks' family competed at International Exhibitions with those produced by the Ransoms and the Sprules, and at the Paris Exhibition in 1867 William Perks gained the only Prize Medal for lavender water and captured the international market, his lavender water becoming the favourite of the Americans. Four years later his son purchased a shop and in 1876 went into partnership with Charles Llewellyn. They styled themselves as 'lavender farmers, peppermint growers and distillers of flowers for essences tinctures etc.'. Lavender was still grown on the outskirts of the town on about 60 acres, when at harvest time it took three weeks for the crop to be processed. Stills were filled four times a day, employees worked from summer dawn to 10 p.m. when lavender pervaded the air, often very strong and coarse in odour. It was the shop manager Richard Lewis who piloted the business following the deaths of both partners and Miss Violet Lewis, the benefactor of the museum piece (see p. 117), followed him. Lavender is no longer cultivated on a commercial scale in Hitchin, but the town honours its lavender history.

Decline

A reduction in the demand for home-produced oils, coupled with rising costs contributed to the decline of the physic gardens trade at the end of the nineteenth century and during the first decade of the twentieth. Further old methods of both cultivation and distilling were adhered to, so that when in the 1880s disease spread among the Mitcham area plants, the price of English produced lavender oil escalated with the resulting loss of market. The USA continued faithfully to buy on the English market, lavender products in particular, but others, the English merchants included bought elsewhere. While English oil of lavender, extracted from plants grown under grey skies in a moderate climate, was always acknowledged to be superior; so was the price! A lack of attention to advancing scientific knowledge especially where the composition of oils was concerned and the adherence to outmoded methods of cultivation were contributing factors to the decline of this rural industry.

An additional reason for the decline in English physic farms generally was that the increased sophistication of synthetic organic chemistry, especialy in the pharmaceutical industry, made possible the production of man-made drugs and perfumes of controlled composition. Imported dried herbs and oils, particularly from Germany and south-eastern Europe replaced home-produced supplies with devastating consequence once war was declared in 1914.

CHELSEA PHYSIC GARDEN

In 1829 came the innovation to open the gates of Chelsea Physic Garden in London to all students of medicine. Great names in horticulture had by now been associated with the garden; William Curtis who launched the *Botanical Magazine*; William Ayton, later of Kew, had trained under Philip Miller; John Fothergill; Robert Fortune, and in mid-century Nathaniel Ward was a curator there. He is famous for inventing the Wardian

Case which allowed plants to be brought undamaged from all corners of the world in constant moisture and temperature. By that time the garden was used for research into medicinal plants by no fewer than 500 medical students a year. How gratified the early apothecaries would have been to know that their struggle to establish and maintain the garden for just such a purpose had been fulfilled.

The Chelsea Physic Garden also became 'old-fashioned' during the last two or three decades of the nineteenth century, primarily because of the change of emphasis in medical training away from physic plants or botany. By 1899 when the maintenance had become an acute financial burden to the Society of Apothecaries it was taken over by the Trustees of the London Parochial Charities and administered by a Committee of Management which included an heir of Sir Hans Sloane, the garden's benefactor 180 years earlier. Improvements were made to the buildings, the valuable library of books was restored which earlier in the nineteenth century had gone to the Apothecaries' Hall, and with renewed purpose the Chelsea Physic Garden was launched into a fresh phase of its useful existence.

HERBALISM

Following a generation of parliamentary discussion, the Medical Act of 1858 established new standards of education for medical students and constituted the formation of The Medical Council. Six years later with the collaboration of the Pharmaceutical Society the first *British Pharmacopoeia* was published. In the same year, 1864, The National Institute of Medical Herbalists was established, and today is the oldest body of medical herbalists in existence. As the pharmaceutical industry progressed during the second half of the century, new drugs could be isolated from plants, and some manufactured synthetically. One well-known example relates to the discovery of salicylic acid in 1838 by a French chemist investigating the active medicinal element of the willow (*Salix alba*). He succeeded in fact to isolate salicin from meadowsweet (then called *Spiraea ulmaria*). Not until 1899 was acetyl-salicylic acid or aspirin synthesized and named after the meadowsweet's German name *Spirinsaure*. The employment of Aspirin for aches and pains allied to rheumatism and for feverish headaches lends powerful credence to the arcane use of meadowsweet for the same ailments. Yet violent purges and emetics, together with blood letting, remained the favoured tools of Victorian medicine while the developing pharmaceutical companies concentrated upon synthetic processes that were to banish many native plants from the medicine chest.

GARDEN PLOTS

Speculate as we will, from inconclusive evidence, no records remain of herbs being cultivated for the greater part of the century, apart from those in kitchen gardens. No doubt cottagers grew their favourites cheek by jowl with the hollyhocks, pinks and Canterbury bells, kale, onions and beans; they were so obviously mundane as to pass unrecorded. In smarter gardens, a vogue developed for individual gardens — an American garden, a heather garden, a fern garden — never a garden for decorative herbs. Herbs came to be considered as remnants of former gardens, or as physic plants.

As flower-garden styles developed towards the later years of the century, the cottage and natural styles gained in popularity as herbaceous borders, wild gardens and rock work, but rarely it seems as herb gardens, and yet these plants were the very breath of the countryside. As the century closed the countryside provided the backdrop for many social activities and for a new style of gardening, yet the herbs held a very minor role in both the front and back stage of people's lives.

Sources of herbs for gardens

Today, herbs are familiar garden plants widely available on every market, at country shows, garden centres, roadside stalls as well as from the nurserymen and seedsmen. But a couple of generations ago it was a very different picture.

Early in the twentieth century, the countryside provided the main source of herbs as plants for the would-be herb gardener. Seedsmen offered a limited range of culinary herbs; Carters of Raynes Park, for example, listed 13 in their *Vade Me Cum* 1901: seed of balm, sweet basil, capsicum, chervil, fennel, marjoram, sage, summer savory, sorrel, thyme and roots at 6d each of mint, horseradish and tarragon. Parlsey was offered separately in eight varieties and described as 'best for garnishing' and of 'special value as an ornamental foliage plant for table decoration and the flower border'. In 1908 The Royal Horticultural Society ran a trial for parsley that resulted in seven Awards of Merit.

E. T. Cook, editor of *Garden*, writing in 1908 proclaimed that it was easier to assemble a good collection of roses or 'the finest and rarest' bulbs, herbaceous plants or orchids than it was to obtain herbs. Frances Bardswell described in 1911 how she acquired the 10 different mints she grew. Some were exchanged with cottage gardeners, corn mint (*Mentha arvensis*) was sought on the edges of cornfields, white woolly mint (*M. sylvestris*) had to be hunted in damp waste places. The round-leaved mint (*M. rotundifolia*) was 'much more difficult to find'. Her plants of lemon mint (*M. citrata*) and curly-leaved mint (*M. crispus*) were presents, peppermint (*M. × piperita*) was 'sent by mistake' and a variegated mint she bought. Of water mint (*M. aquatica*) she says 'required no looking for. Does it not throw itself at our feet . . . by river banks and watery meadows?' Spear or lamb mint (*M. spicata*) grew 'as a matter of course in every well-regulated garden'.

Decorative herb gardens

By no means were herbs teetering on the brink of extinction at the turn of the present century; after all, some were common wild flowers. Others, like parsley, sage, chives and mint were offered widely by the nurserymen and seedsmen, and squandered themselves in kitchen gardens. Other herbs such as lavender, rosemary, thyme, mallow, southernwood and marjoram inhabited the flower garden. Some were what William Robinson called 'old garden plants', violet, sea holly, santolina and balm. (He decried borage). Devotees made personal collections of Shakespeare's flowers dotted with decorative labels with appropriate quotations. A Parkinson Society was formed whose members dedicated themselves to tracking down the plants he had described in the seventeenth century, many of them old herbs.

'Old-fashioned gardens' enjoyed a vogue, sparked by Tennyson, especially newly created ones in public parks where some herbs were included for decoration. (Today we may call this garden restoration or recreation and we indulge in horticultural backward glances with increasing pre-occupation.) The Arts and Crafts Movement fostered a popularity for economic herbs especially as dye plants: William Morris and others sought inspiration from the plant world for many designs.

Such self-indulgent gardeners of the 1890s as The Countess of Warwick had 'A Border of Sentiment' where 'the dear old herbs and flowers' were labelled with 'quaint meanings and emblems of bygone times'. Each label was a swallow in form, the flower name on one wing, the emblem on the other: balm plant of sympathy, basil plant of hatred, bay leaves for glory, the heartsease for waiting and hemp for fate. Her garden at Stone Hall at her home, Easton Lodge in Essex, is one of the few of the period in which individual plants were recorded, and we find some herbs collected there in decorative borders. The Shakespeare border for example culled many of them, of which more than 50 would be considered as herbs proper today. Clearly there was no suggestion that herbs *per se* should be cultivated together.

It is not surprising to find some resistance to bringing herbs out of the kitchen garden and planting them for fun. Francis Bardswell in her book *The Herb Garden* (1911) says that the best herb borders were in kitchen gardens 'of people who keep a chef'. She goes on 'Though not grown in any way for ornament many of these unpretending Herb-borders look quite fascinating; bees and butterflies hover over them and spicy fragrances are wafted from them that remind one of the Maritime Alps'. She reports that her gardening friends say 'I would never care for a Herb-garden, you cannot make it pretty'. Chervil, burnet, purslane, betony, herb patience, Good King Henry, smallage, lovage and pepperwort she lists as being rarely seen at that time and the gardens illustrated in her book depict only herb borders.

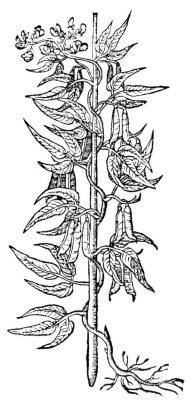

Gertrude Jekyll

That Miss Jekyll, who relished everything natural and countrywise did not pay homage in her plans to the herbs perhaps seems surprising. She loved santolina and lavender, and used rosemary and pinks in her border designs, yet her three or four herb garden plans appear to have been perfunctory exercises and may well, as at Boveridge, have been requested by the owners, and at Bunningford been a kitchen herb border. Scented gardens held greater appeal for her. She prepared the plans, for example, for the Rosemary Garden at King Edward VII Sanatorium at Midhurst, Sussex. The planting was carried out by the young ladies from the Glynde School of Gardening, run by Frances Garnet, Viscountess Wolseley.

While the fervour invoked by the Jekyllian spirit straddled into every large garden and country estate, Reginald Blomfield's *The Formal Garden* (1901) pleaded for the clarity of rigid design, fuelling strong opposition. In their combined masterpiece at Hestercombe, near Taunton, Somerset, Lutyens and Jekyll provided the answer. Edwin Lutyens' highly geometrical plats, pergola and various levels were softened by Miss Jekyll's blousy planting. Had modern photocopy reductions been available, the smaller plan of the great plat at Hestercombe *might* just have suggested planting with the dainty leaved and transient flowers of herbs. Then the formal herb garden may have evolved. Perhaps here is a further clue, for the Edwardians indulged themselves with lavish gardens, seeking colour especially late in the season and took to their hearts the new late-flowering roses and dahlias and Michaelmas daisies. With herbs the season is short. Furthermore, in the late nineteenth and early twentieth centuries, the nurserymen were feverishly introducing new cultivars, and in the search for spectacular effect understandably the herbs were overlooked.

Miss Jekyll first brought herbs through the garden gate (just!) when in 1907 she designed a small formal quincunx beneath the kitchen garden wall at Knebworth House in Hertfordshire. Her 'design' was in fact a replanting scheme for an existing Victorian flower bed and it seems highly probable that it was done as a birthday present for a member of the Cobhold family into which her friend Edwin Lutyens had married. That little design had to wait until the 1980s to be planted! Other early herb garden plans of Jekyll's were for Barrington Court, Somerset (1917), Boveridge House, Dorset (1920) and Bunningfold, Surrey (1923). Scant evidence of any of them ever being planted confirms the lack-lustre appeal of herbs at that time. Each plan was merely a set of rectangular blocks formed along the border suggesting fewer than 10 or 15 kinds of herbs in all.

Other designers such as Thomas Mawson and Avery Tipping relished exuberant planting to provide masses of bold colour within a formal setting, so the gentle herbs simply did not come into the picture. Even J. D. Sedding who professed that the old-fashioned gardens were part of the 'quiet beautiful life of bygone times' did not include herbs in the schemes he proffered.

Contemporary resistance to herbs stemmed from the abandoning of herbalism in the nineteenth century and it was only writers such as Gertrude Jekyll who advocated herb borders as part of the kitchen garden. Apart from their rare appearance in clipped proclamations, such as Ye Herb Garden at Broughton Castle, Oxfordshire at the turn of the century, herbs were usually grown in informal borders in the 'cottage' style. 'Strangely few care to possess Herb Gardens now, being either careless, or forgetful of their delicate charms and preferring some brilliant growth' wrote M. R. Gload in 1906.

Some gardens obviously escaped description and photographic record; not so the Lavender and Herb Garden at Ashridge, Hertfordshire. Probably because of the monastic foundation of the site, Lady Brownlow had a herb garden as a further individual scheme within the garden as a whole, famous for a series of small gardens. The centre piece was an armillary sphere which remained until the early 1970s (when it was stolen) surrounded by a circular bed of lavender clasped by outer semi-circular beds and in which a variety of herbs were planted. Sweet basil, burnet, thyme, rue, mint, sage, tansy, rosemary, pennyroyal, and fennel were there, each accompanied by 'their names quaintly cut besides them in the terra cotta edging'. Two older arbours in the form of 'houses' stood at the side, to form what must have been a formal herb garden enclosed and set in the lawn. The two 'houses' remain.

An Edwardian herb border in June, watercolour by Isabelle Forrest, depicts informal borders planted with (back to front) caraway, tarragon, rue, mint, parsley, sage, thyme, purple sage, chives and thyme. (R back to front) lemon balm, sorrel, borage, chamomile, alkanet and pot marigold.

Another exception to the rule was manifest in the Elizabethan herb garden at Friar Park near Henley, Oxfordshire, but then fantastic exceptions to most gardening rules found a home there! The herb garden Sir Frank Crisp laid out followed a plan from Hyll's *Gardeners Labyrinth* (1571). Beds were raised and supported by boards in older style and medicinal herbs planted in one half of the garden and flowers 'for use rather than Beauty' in the other. The list is the most extensive of the period (*c.* 1910).

Medicinal Plants and Flowers in the Elizabethan Herb Garden at Friar Park

Medicinal Plants		Medicinal Flowers	
angelica	hyssop	all heal	orpine
anise	liquorice	candytuft	paeony
asarabacca	lovage	clove pink	primrose
balm	marjoram	columbine	rampion
borage	mugwort	comfrey	saffon thistle
burnet	penny royal	dog rose	St. John's wort
bush basil	purslane	dog's tooth violet	sea holly
caraway	rue	fraxinella	snap dragon
catmint	sea purslane	golden rod	Solomon's seal
clary	sorrel	hearts ease	sweet violet
coriander	summer savory	iris (*germanica*)	wallflower
dill	sweet cicely	jacob's ladder	white damask rose
dragons (tarragon)	vervain	larkspur	white lily
elecampane	vipers grass	lily-of-the-valley	winter cherry
germander	winter savory	mandrake	woad
good King Henry	wormwood	marigold	wood sorrel
horehound		monkswood	yellow gentian

The Edwardians expressed their enthusiasm for gardens in watercolours in which flowers bloomed in unison and the sun was always shining. Isabelle Forrest portrayed a herb garden with (from back to front) red and white valerian, fumitory, cat mint, santolina and woodruff.

MAUD GRIEVE

Sophia Emma Magdalene Law was born in Islington on 4 May 1858 and always used the name Maud because she disliked her Christian names so much. As a young girl she married William Sommerville Grieve, her elder by many years, and went out to India with him, where they lived until his retirement. Together they made a remarkable collection of Indian Art, some of which was lent for the Calcutta Exhibition in 1884, on which occasion Maud Grieve won a prize for an oil painting of an Indian street scene. (Until recently the painting hung in Buckinghamshire alongside her exquisitely carved teak painting cabinet which her husband commissioned for her.)

Shortly after their return to England they settled at The Whins, Chalfont St Peter, Buckinghamshire (*c.* 1908), a house designed to be labour-saving by her husband. There Maud Grieve set about making a garden and engaging in urban life. (Some of her neighbours were the Townsend sisters, one to become a famous gardener, Margery Fish.)

From about 1908 when she started making her garden at The Whins, Maud Grieve grew herbs and vegetable drugs and supplied manufacturing chemists. It may be that her interest had been aroused in connection with a medical mission in Calcutta with which she had been involved. Quickly she lent her support to various women's agricultural and horticultural movements in which the main objectives were to gain the acceptance of trained women. No evidence is forthcoming to indicate that she received any training in horticulture but she was in touch with two or three people who ran gardening schools for young ladies and she became a member of The Daughters of Ceres. Ostensibly, this was the former students' guild for women who had trained at The Lady Warwick Hostel at Reading and Studley College, Warwickshire, to which ladies working in an accepted field were enlisted. Mrs Grieve became the Buckinghamshire County Representative for the movement in 1911. Some members were to lend weight to a number of 'women on the land' enterprises during the 1914–1918 war. During the War also, Maud Grieve was to collaborate closely with E. M. Holmes.

In 1911 E. M. Holmes, President of the Pharmaceutical Society addressed the Royal Commission on the Resources and Trade of the Dominions, suggesting that a Bureau of Plant Industry might be established in England. The Conference was told that dill seed, coriander, fennel and henbane were worthy of increased attention and Sir Rider Haggard made the point that essential oil crops could be produced by smallholders. Herbalists still flourished, especially in country districts and the north, and offered a market to growers of herbs. E. M. Holmes tried to persuade the Government, especially during the War, that the estuaries of Poole Harbour could, if improved, provide 50 square miles for herbs and drug cultivation.

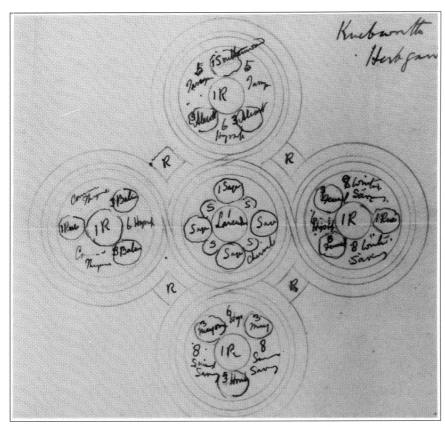

A small Victorian style bedding scheme just outside the kitchen garden wall at Knebworth House, Hertfordshire (opposite) was Gertrude Jekyll's inspiration for a herb garden. In 1907 she designed a replanting scheme using herbs. The plan lay unused until 1982 when it was carried out by Mike Calnan during the restoration of the garden at Knebworth House. (See also text on p. 81.)

VI

SPOTLIGHT ON HERBS
(1915 onwards)

*From Saxon days until the end of the eighteenth century the herb-garden
reigned supreme in England, and now that we are reviving so much
that is old and pleasant, perhaps we shall be wise enough to restore the
herb-garden with its beautiful colours and its fragrance to its former
pride of place.*

Eleanour Sinclair Rohde, The Scented Garden *(1932)*

The golden glow of Edwardian-style gardens, in which the sun seems always to have
been shining, faded with the 1914–1918 War and a far more 'down to earth' attitude
towards all things horticultural prevailed. Whereas in the past it had always been men
who had made gardens and run nurseries, the examples of Gertrude Jekyll and Ellen
Willmott together with the various women's pioneering organizations, including those
devoted to the land, provided a seed ground for women to surface as garden writers,
designers and above all owners of plant nurseries and smallholdings. 'Luxury herbs', as
the delicate scented conceits of the inter-war years were called, were designed for ladies,
and after World War II it seemed apposite to indulge in the 'old pleasaunt' gardens.
Simultaneously, the potentiality of plants as sources of medicine was being reappraised
not only by the pharmaceutical multinationals, but in academic circles and various far-
reaching organizations such as the World Health Organization. A need was recognized
to retain some plants for study as well as to renew investigative pharmacognosy. Natural
medicines, alternative doctrines for healing, relaxation and aromatherapy, and
vegetarianism captured popular interest. Together with the back-to-peaceful-nature
movement which peaked in the flower power of the 1960s, an amalgam of ideas and
ideals surfaced which turned the spotlight on to herbs, first perhaps in a folksy way, but
for the gardeners in a way that allowed olden wisdom to become a buzz maxim.
Throughout the 1970s and 1980s, herb gardens were created, as fabulous and as
curious to present-day gardeners as former ones had been for John Gerard and John
Parkinson.

When war was declared in August 1914, the Board of Agriculture and Fisheries
issued a bulletin (No. 288) *The Cultivation and Collection of Medicinal Plants in
England*, dealing with the wartime emergency because the bulk of vegetable drugs were
imported from the European mainland, Germany, Austria and the Balkans in
particular. Mrs Grieve was one of the civilians who responded to the request to raise
medicinal herbs together with the owners of many country houses, cottagers and spare
acres. Soon it was apparent that a well-organized system of collection and drying of the
herbs had to be established and linked in to the work of E. M. Holmes at The
Pharmaceutical Society. Maud Grieve became the motivating luminary for much of that
work and was asked by the Government to train pupils. Here lay her real life's work,
although she was then in her mid-fifties.

Immediately Maud Grieve set up her training school at The Whins, and expanded the
area under cultivation. Old hop-drying sheds in which to dry herbs were acquired and
the whole organization expanded. Her helper was Miss Oswald, a 'Medalist of the
Society of Apothecaries' (although they have no record of her name). Residential
students lived at The Whins Cottage, a small house on the farm, in addition to which
there were many day classes and a correspondence course. Maud Grieve demonstrated,
taught and organized 'herborizing' expeditions into the Buckinghamshire countryside
to teach plant identification, in much the same way that Thomas Johnson had done
early in the seventeenth century.

Maud Grieve working on her correspondence in the 1920s in her office at The Whins. Each pigeon hole held copies of one of the pamphlets on herbs which later were published as A Modern Herbal *(1931).*

THE NATIONAL HERB-GROWING ASSOCIATION

Maud Grieve was instrumental in inaugurating the National Herb-Growing Association, in conjunction with the Women's Farm and Garden Union (now Association), and began to issue pamphlets of individual herbs in some detail. 'I began to master the subject', she wrote; 'After lecturing and demonstrating all day, I would sit up half the night reading up all the authorities'; and, 'Museums have been researched, the results of the labour of the Agricultural Departments incorporated, the practical working described, thus giving a complete history of each individual plant, and the whole is expressed in simple language which (except to editors and publishers) may at first sight, not render apparent the immense amount of work expended on their preparation'.

Leaflets — or pamphlets as she called them — were distributed in addition to home-produced seed, by mail order; the walls of her office at The Whins were lined with pigeon holes in which leaflets and seed were arranged. The availability of the various leaflets was announced in the W. F. & G. U. leaflet and cost 2d to members or 1/6 per dozen to branches or Groups. The National Herb-Growing Association's headquarters were at Queen Anne's Chambers, Westminster and Mr Wolfe acted as Secretary throughout the War. To allay the faint-hearted who voiced the opinion that herb-growing and collecting would be a lost labour, appeals for herbs were published from Belgium and from 'business firms' to reinforce the needs for herbs and vegetable drugs, and to stimulate interest.

The entire movement became known as one of Britain's 'invisible industries' and had an extraordinary early success with Groups organized in many widely dispersed areas of

The first herb garden to be exhibited at Chelsea Flower Show in May 1919 was arranged by Maud Grieve (seated) and Eleanour Sinclair Rohde.

the country, each with a herb-drying centre. It is reported to have 'failed' as a result of 'too many departments under one organizer'. In other words it became too difficult to administer. Nearer the truth perhaps is that a war-weary band of volunteers found the remuneration for collecting herbs and vegetable drugs unsatisfactory. More forceful, perhaps was the mistaken euphoria and emotion that attended the idea of herbs.

Edith Hughes and luxury herbs

At the time it was disbanded the most efficient of the Groups with drying sheds was run by Miss Edith Hughes at Chester in Cheshire. She had been one of Mrs Grieve's pupils at The Whins, and she and her enthusiastic band of helpers carried on for a further year. Collectors became dissatisfied with their remuneration and the prices the drug firms offered for belladonna, henbane, dandelion, marigold petals and opium poppy represented a turnover of about £250, which the expenses exceeded. Edith Hughes continued to cultivate herbs and relocated to a small herb farm in Sussex and in her determination to make the enterprise pay, opened a tiny shop in Brighton. Mail order sales followed, as 'The Green-Harvest Industry', she developed what were then known as 'luxury herbs' — lavender, sweet conceits, hair tonics and pot pourri. The medicinal herb-growing and marketing were handed over to another lady herbalist. Edith Hughes promoted herbal toilet preparations, scented articles and pot pourri from stands at a wide range of exhibitions and trade fairs following the War and during the early 1920s, and she was the pioneer of the 'luxury herbs' retail trade. Her enterprising ideas were adopted by Dorothy Hewer at The Herb Shop and by Hilda Leyel in the Culpeper House chain of shops both started in the mid-1920s.

THE BRITISH GUILD OF HERB GROWERS

About the time the National Herb-Growers Association was disbanded, the British Guild of Herb Growers was inaugurated (1918) with Mrs Grieve as President. To celebrate the first anniversary and to publicize her work, she took a stand at Chelsea Flower Show in May 1919 where she was helped by Eleanour Sinclair Rohde. We can

only speculate that the membership of the Guild included one or two enthusiasts from the Herb-Growing Association and some former students from The Whins and no doubt those who ran nurseries at Aberystwyth and Swansea. Other notable growers were Mr Allder of Leighton Buzzard, Mr Seymour of Halbeach and Messrs Flemons & Kerry of Dunstable.

The preparation of dried herbs at Maud Grieve's establishment at Chalfont St Peter, Buckinghamshire about 1920 in 'the outer room or the herb drying house'.

At that time the drying sheds at The Whins were considered to be the finest in the country and Maud Grieve pressed on relentlessly with her teaching and demonstrating and constantly updated her pamphlets 'to keep in touch with the latest developments of science'.

When the War ended she continued and expanded her work, training ex-servicemen, some of whom were destined to cultivate vegetable drugs in the colonies. She worked with Sam Ryder who together with two brothers founded Heath and Heather for the sale of herbal products in 1924. One of her pupils was Eleanour Sinclair Rohde. There is a very faded photograph of Mrs Grieve demonstrating the propagation of chamomile to a group of lady students which includes Miss Rohde in 1916. By that time Eleanour Sinclair Rohde had begun her study of traditional plants and herbals and was already gardening at her house in Reigate.

'The Movement initiated during the War', Maud Grieve said, 'has placed us in a position to provide the wants of trades and professions of all kinds — doctors, veterinary surgeons, chemists and druggists, perfumers, dyers, confectioners and manufacturers of many essential commodities'. She encouraged colonial herb-farming, sending peppermint and lavender plants and clary seed to fruit-growing settlements in Cape Colony, and recommended the cultivation of 'prickly comfrey' (*Symphytum aspermum*) and goat's rue (*Galega officinalis*) for green fodder crops in Africa. She showed a special interest in the production of essential oils and perfume in Australia and two of her ex-servicemen pupils studied essential oils at The Whins before going to farm scented herbs in New South Wales. She conducted experiments in the value of pyrethrum (*Chrysanthemum coccineum*) as an insecticide and pleaded that it be adopted as a commercial crop in the colonies.

Maud Grieve's devotion to the herb world persisted throughout the 1920s; she contributed to a range of journals, updated and reissued her leaflets, while collaborating with Professor Geoffrey Henslow of the Royal Horticultural Society in his book. She still continued to train her students but when her husband's health failed in the late 1920s, she closed her school and much of her herb stock went to The Herb Farm at Seal where Dorothy Hewer was starting up. There is no doubt that this very feminine and indefatigable lady had contributed a great deal towards establishing a herb-growing industry in this country.

THE HERB FARM AT SEAL

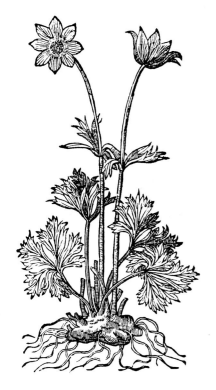

In the mid-1920s (*c.* 1926) Miss Dorothy G. Hewer, a graduate in science and from a family of London doctors, started a herb farm on a hillside near Seal, Kent. A considerable amount of the initial plant stock and 'much needed advice' came from Mrs Grieve; thus the Herb Farm was established with between eight and twelve students. Dorothy Hewer believed passionately in a good healthy outdoor life of work. She concentrated mainly upon the cultivation of lavender for oil of lavender and the production of dried and rubbed medicinal herbs which, together with herb plants and seeds, were marketed by mail order and sold direct from The Herb Shop at 16, North Audley Street, London, opened in 1930.

Owned by Miss Hewer, but subsequently under the aegis of a large company, it was managed by Mrs Maud White, close friend of the garden writer Marion Cran. Here to be found also were packets of mixed herbs for adding to poultry dishes, omelettes, stuffings and so forth, and sachets of moth repellents, clove oranges, herb pillows and all the scented knick-knacks which today are found in every souvenir shop.

Miniature versions of 'Japanese Gardens' comprising dwarf rosemary, hyssop and thyme were another innovation offered for sale. On the farm back in Kent a very wide range of plants were identified and built up so that intending herb gardeners no longer experienced the frustrations Eleanour Sinclair Rohde had complained about just a few years beforehand. At the farm, drying sheds housed 'numerous tiers of large canvas trays, on which freshly harvested herbs were spread'. Heated by special stoves, the sheds required skilled management, since different herbs demand different temperatures for quick drying. Buttercup flowers were dried also, rapidly to preserve their colour, and later added to the pot pourri made on the farm. Certainly in the 1930s children arrived with bags bulging with harvested buttercup flowers and received 4d per pound.

Miss Hewer developed her own strain of lavender known as 'Seal' and generally applied her scientific knowledge and business acumen to promote herb-farming as a worthwhile industry which could compete with foreign trade that supplied what was generally accepted as inferior material at superior prices. She built on the commercial work and training of girls for the industry which Maud Grieve had carried on at The Herb School behind The Whins, which was closed in 1929. The herb industry today owes much to Dorothy Hewer's innovations.

She lectured and demonstrated particularly to Women's Institutes and her book *Practical Herb Growing* (1941) was the first of its kind since Ada Teetgen's *Profitable Herb Growing and Cultivation* (1916), devoted to the cultivation and drying of herbs and became World War II's counterpart to Maud Grieves' pamphlets of World War I. It was written in response to the constant requests Miss Hewer received for cultural information and for years remained the only book of its kind. I had the honour, for so it seemed, of updating it in 1968 after her death.

The Herb Farm exhibited first at Chelsea Flower Show in 1949, after a trial stand of the Royal Horticultural Society's early March show that year. Subsequently they exhibited regularly throughout the 1950s and 1960s, the last Chelsea stand being in 1967. By then the farm was in the hands of Miss Margaret E. Brownlow who had been Miss Hewer's pupil and became her successor. It was Margaret Brownlow who attested a few years later that unless they were on a large scale, herb farms would for ever be unviable economically in England because labour was becoming more expensive and it was difficult to compete with herb farms in warmer climates, with cheaper help. She could not have foreseen the explosion of small herb nurseries during the 1970s and 1980s, churning out herbs for home consumption in answer to domestic demand.

After wandering around the country in search of remedial flowers for some years Edward Bach settled in a simple house in Oxfordshire. Today it remains the centre from which his work is continued.

BACH FLOWER REMEDIES

Much herbal medicine in the past was empirical, interpreting man's raw relationship with plants combined with traditional mythology. Similar convictions linger in the twentieth-century mind, and increasingly so. In the 1920s and 30s, Dr Edward Bach, a respected doctor of medicine specializing in bacteriology devoted the greater part of his time to researching curative plants. During his early career he had gained recognition for developing oral vaccines and subsequently came across the homoeopathic principles of Hahnemann from a century earlier which supported his own independent theories. Since his student days he had studied closely the temperaments of patients, believing passionately that those with a similar personality would respond to the same remedy, while others of a different temperament required some other cure even when suffering from the same complaint. Today this approach of 'the whole person' is accepted far more easily.

Deeply attracted to the open countryside Edward Bach left his remunerative hospital and consultancy work in London to explore the possibility of finding natural healing principles compatible with a range of temperaments and states of mind. He considered, for example, fear, depression, anger or worry, and sought to identify herbs that allayed such inhibiting factors. For some years he lived in dire poverty, pushing himself to the limits of his strength both mental and physical, roaming England in search of plants which he intuitively suspected would fulfil his purpose. He argued that the dew enfolding a plant in the early morning, when warmed by the sun, became infused with the healing principle drawn from the plant. Thus his 'sun method' of producing remedies as naturally as nature itself was developed by soaking the appropriate flowers in spring water and leaving the sun to do the rest. He called it potentizing. Tinctures produced in this way were then stabilized in brandy.

Bach became convinced not only that sun-warmed 'dew' absorbed the essential healing principle of the plant but that the resulting remedies could flood the body with calming and healing vibrations. His treatments became popular especially in North Wales, Cromer and Marlow where he settled temporarily from time to time during his wanderings in search of remedial herbs. The first three he identified were agrimony, chicory and vervain, then followed clematis (*Clematis vitalba*), centaury (*Centaurium minus*) and *Ceratostigma willmottiana* (the only plant among his remedies which does not grow wild in England). An extraordinary inner knowledge led him to establish twelve healers and what he chose to call 'helpers'. The twelve healers were:

clematis	*Clematis vitalba*
agrimony	*Agrimonia eupatoria*
chicory	*Cichorium intybus*
vervain	*Verbena officinalis*
centaury	*Centaurium minus*
cerato	*Ceratostigma willmottiana*
balsam	*Impatiens roylei*
knawlweed	*Scleranthus annuus*
musk	*Mimulus luteus*
water violet	*Hottonia palustris*
autumn gentian	*Gentianella amarella*
rock rose	*Helianthemum chamaecistus*

Further plants were researched and included, some known as 'helpers' although the system of herbal medicine is now known as 'The Twelve Healers'.

By the early 1930s, amid increased popularity for his treatments and his own highly sensitized convictions, he was threatened by the General Medical Council with the erasure of his name from the Medical Register, for not only were his methods unorthodox but, horror of horrors he was advertising! He seems not to have heeded such threats and in order to make available his simple remedies to the public at large he gave mother-tinctures to two London chemists.

A further range of plants, some recognized herbs, others such as honeysuckle, were included in later treatments and Bach's remedies and writing remain popular today, the guiding principles closely akin to various fields of alternative medicine. Edward Bach provided a powerful link with the arcane four humours upon which Medieval medicine depended and the consideration of the whole person in medical parlance today. Moreover, like Culpeper before him, he sought to simplify herbal treatment and make them freely available to everyone.

THE SOCIETY OF HERBALISTS

Meanwhile through the 1920s an independent spirit was working in the world of herbalism developing her own spiritual methods of natural healing. Hilda Winifred Wauton was born at Uppingham, Rutland, in 1880 where her father was a school housemaster. She married, when she was 20 years old, a Swedish theatrical manager and became Mrs C. F. Leyel — a name that was to become well known in pre-war Society as a pretty and capable hostess, and afterwards for her work in herbal astrological counselling and pioneering several causes. In the early 1920s as a result of her efforts to generate funds for charities supporting ex-servicemen and hospitals she organized the Golden Ballot. Some £350 000 were raised, and she was prosecuted for her activity in this concern. Eventually she was acquitted, thereby legalizing such ballots for charity. However, it was in her dedication to herbs, vegetable drugs and healing that she sought to promote understanding.

Herbs and potent medicines had been dubbed the stuff of quacks and Hilda Leyel argued that proven herbal treatment had existed before germs were recognized and that a healthy holistic approach was a harmonious route to healing. Quite independently she launched the Society of Herbalists in 1927. Her consulting rooms were at 10, Baker

Street, where a reputable private practice was built up. The 'shop window' was provided by the Culpeper House enterprise, the first shop for which was opened at the same time in Bruton Street, London.

Her eight books on herbs were erudite, although somewhat offbeat at the time of publication during the 1940s, but nevertheless gained considerable popularity. Known as the Culpeper House Books or the Faber Herbals they still reside on many bookshelves and were the precursors of the spate of books on the subject of herbs over the ensuing 40 years. Mrs Leyel wrote also on cookery and culinary matters.

Culpeper House

Hilda Leyel was supported from the inception of the Society of Herbalists by an Advisory Committee of influential friends. In fact up to the outbreak of World War II in 1939, the committee harked back to the Edwardian style of 'well-connected' people as patrons of the Society. Eleanour Sinclair Rohde, Dame Edith Sitwell and the composer Eric Coates were each committee members by 1939. The country-green façade of the Culpeper Shops, the first interior of which was designed by Basil Ionides (another committee member) and their informative catalogues, achieved great popularity throughout the ensuing 30 years. Culpeper House became synonymous with 'country' fragrances, natural cosmetics, natural food and herbal remedies and did much to popularize all such products readily available today. Shops were opened in all the fashionable towns including Dublin in Ireland, in much the same way that the Body Shop followed during the 1980s. Culpeper House remains a progressive company.

Hilda Leyel's powerful commitment to natural healing alerted her to fight for some freedom to practise herbal medicine when in 1941 The Pharmacy and Medicines Bill threatened to destroy the legal practice of herbal medicine in England. With support from some of her influential friends the Bill was eventually amended to allow treatment to be given to patients who became members of The Society of Herbalists. In hindsight it is clear that her efforts at that time, 1941, left the door open for the acceptance of herbal treatment as an alternative of complementary medicine. Today new negotiations are being sought in establishing the position within the EC. Herbal medicines on the continent of Europe are monopolized by the pharmacies, who are obviously reluctant to relinquish their control.

A wealth of Herbals

Hilda Leyel's collection of herbals, and the exquisite flower books that had replaced them, was one of the finest privately owned in the country. A selection from it was displayed at Londonderry House, Park Lane, London in 1953 as an Exhibition of Flower Books from the Library of the Society of Herbalists and was sponsored by The Arts Council. For many visitors to that exhibition it was a revelation, and for me it provided the tinder that fired a life-long interest in herbs and herbals. From the works of Dioscorides in a twelfth-century manuscript copy through numerous European herbals, some of which had been translated into English in their day, we were taken to Mark Catesby's thrilling accounts of the natural history of Carolina in which he paid considerable attention to herbs and other useful plants. Then some of the luscious flower portraits of Sowerby's English plants at the turn of the century, and Thornton's *Temple of Flora* of the same period. The mid-nineteenth century hunger for exotic decorative plants cultivated in our gardens was appeased by Sydenham Edwards *The Botanical Register* and Lindley's monograph on roses. Roses appeared again in Alfred Parsons' exquisite rose portraits in Ellen Willmott's *The Genus Rosa* published just prior to the 1914–18 war. John Nash's *English Flower Garden* with modern lithographs contemporary with the exhibition brought the story up to date.

THE HERB SOCIETY

Following Mrs Leyel's death five years after the exhibition, the herbals were bequeathed to the Society of Herbalists, but alas lengthy litigation ensued and some misunderstanding of which volumes were specifically herbals. Some books were auctioned at Sotheby's, the Society receiving only £2000, a small percentage of the proceeds. Up to

Culpeper House products increased in popularity and appeal immediately before and after World War II. A design by Beryl Hodge for the 1951 catalogue promotes floral preparations.

One of the many successful herb nurseries established during the 1970s and 1980s is Hollington Nurseries, near Newbury, Berkshire. From the beginning it was laid out as a garden to demonstrate the decorative qualities of herbs.

that time the Society of Herbalists and Culpeper House had been a joint concern, the latter an expensive undertaking. By 1967, in an attempt to prevent the demise of the retail establishments, the remaining herbals from the Society's Library were auctioned, again at Sotheby's. Even the resultant fund of £65 000 did little to relieve the long-term prospects, so the name and goodwill of Culpeper shops were separated from the Society, which in turn 10 years later adopted the title of The Herb Society and became a registered educational charity.

No longer the mouthpiece of the medical herbalists, it, like many herb gardens, has its sequestered periods and its periods of high profile. Some of the exhibits the Society has organized at Chelsea Flower Show, for example, have made lively conversation for herb lovers – not least the competition winner's garden in 1977 designed by Leslie Bremens, who went on to write a tome on herbs and herbal delights followed by a more fanciful TV series on herbs in the late 1980s. Others that caught public attention, if only to ask how Elizabethan Knot Gardens came to be Japanese and/or American, were those prettily contrived by Terry Stratton and Tessa Traeger for a subsequent Herb Society exhibit.

HERB FARMING

During the years between the wars the commercial cultivation of herbs declined, although during the early 1930s a revival of interest in rural industries led to a reawakening awareness of herbs. The (then) Ministry of Agriculture advised that information should be sought from the National Federation of Women's Institutes 'or in some counties, such as Warwickshire from the Country Education Authorities'.

Farms and small holdings cultivating herbs during the 1930s included areas of Middlesex, Essex, Kent, Worcestershire, Bedfordshire and the Midlands for parsley. (It was estimated at the turn of the present century that more than 600 tons (13 44 000 kg) of parsley was the average amount sent from Bedfordshire to Glasgow!). Important mint-producing areas included Cheshire and Cambridge together with local activity centred around Cheltenham, Bristol and Wakefield. Sage-growing required drier conditions and was carried on in Cambridgeshire, Kent, Surrey and Bedfordshire; the

Hollington Nurseries today where the policy continues to prove the versatility of herbs as garden-worthy plants.

same areas produced thyme although the main supplies were imported as dried thyme from Germany. Fennel appeared on market stalls in the north Midlands, and sorrel was grown on small-holdings in Middlesex. Forced chervil appeared in Covent Garden Market from time to time.

Medicinal herbs produced in the UK were cultivated mainly on drug farms owned or supported by the pharmaceutical companies. Some with belladonna and henbane grew in Bedfordshire, Hertfordshire and Oxfordshire; licorice remained exclusive to the Pontefract district of Yorkshire where the Black Friars had started to grow it in the sixteenth century. Valerian cultivation still centred upon Derbyshire; aconite and foxglove were cropped regularly on the drug farms of Hertfordshire and Bedfordshire. Rhubarb remained a local crop of the Banbury area as it had been for more than a century.

However, the drug manufacturers of the UK relied heavily upon imported supplies and once again found themselves cut off from their Continental sources during World War II. Once again official appeals were made for the collection of wild plants. The wholesale druggists Brome & Schimmer issued a booklet entitled *Herb Growing* (1941) written by Barbara Keen and Jean Armstrong in which they gave of their professional knowledge on the part of the plant to collect, when to harvest and advice on how to dry over 60 herbs.

HERB NURSERIES AND PRIVATE ENTERPRISE

Barbara Keen is now very well known among herbalists and has been growing herbs since 1932 when she launched on her career as one of Miss Hewer's students at Seal. First her commercial venture took her to Llanymynech in North Wales where she grew and dried medicinal herbs for the wholesale drug market through W. H. Allden of Linslade, Buckinghamshire, who dried, processed and washed great quantities of herbs from the wild and formulated tonics during the War. Having married in 1939, Mrs Keen began growing herbs at her home in Shropshire where she established Valeswood Herb Farm. There was little competition in the early years, other herb nurseries included Petals and Herbs at Stoke by Clare, Suffolk, run by Mrs Kitty Champion and

Margaret Brownlow of the Herb Farm, Seal, Kent, expressed her creative talents and love of herbs in her writing and gardens, but above all in her painting.

Ashfield Herb Farm near Market Drayton, Shropshire, which belonged to Mr and Mrs Evette where they included several American homoeopathic plants. Edwin and Anette Evette took over a piece of land in 1967 which had not been farmed for a century, but curiously the deeds revealed that it had been owned, and presumably farmed, in 1809, by John Nicholls, an apothecary. Madge Hooper, who had been secretary to Miss Hewer at Seal, set up Stoke Lacy, Bromyard. The herb farm at Tumblers Bottom near Radstock, Avon, was run by Guy Cooper and Gordon Taylor who subsequently moved to London to administer the Herb Society when Dr Malcolm Stuart left.

By the mid-1970s, some garden centres began to stock herbs and other farms began, several in a small way. Clare Lowenfeld ran Chiltern Herbs, one of the first to produce supermarket packets of dried herbs at Chartridge, Hertfordshire, reputedly on land where Mrs Grieve had grown herbs while The Whins was being built. Peter Wimperis began The Selsley Herb and Goat Farm at Stroud, Gloucestershire; Reginald and Elizabeth Peplow flourished at Herbs from the Hoo near Huntingdon, Cambridgeshire; Iden Croft Nurseries, at Staplehurst, Kent; Wells & Winter of Maidstone, Kent; Netherfield Herbs, Roughham, Suffolk; Herbs in Stock, at Stock, Essex. Daphne Ffiske had a nursery near Norwich, Norfolk, and Jill Davies, a qualified medical herbalist, embarked upon her herbal teas and other remedies at Thornham Herbs at Eye, Suffolk. An energetic crop of growers and tiny nurseries germinated in response to the demand for herbal delights, fresh herbs and above all herb plants to furnish the burgeoning interest in herb gardens. Never before in the history of horticulture has there been such a proliferation of herb nurseries. After more than 40 years of attempting to bring the growers together, Barbara Keen successfully launched The Association of British Herb Growers and Producers in 1976, which became The British Herb Traders Association in 1981.

Hollington Nurseries Ltd

As an example of the broadening vogue for herbs, Simon and Judith Hopkinson, who grow and market herbs at Hollington, Berkshire, have found their market extending. They now supply plants of fresh herbs to supermarkets, garden centres, local authorities, landscape architects in addition to private individuals. It was in 1976 that they began their enterprise within a 1½ acre (0.6 hectares) walled garden, erecting tunnels, buying in stock, and propagating plants so that two years later the gates were opened for business to the general public. Nine years later a new site of some 2½ acres (1.1 hectares) was added for wholesale plants and in spite of losing four tunnels in the 1981 storm, tunnels and glass houses are continually being added and replaced, as after the storm damage of 1989–90. By 1990 they employed eight people, supplemented in spring and summer by a further four or five. Constantly stock is sought, particularly to amend their lists, from Europe as well as from the UK. Most of the stock is built up at Hollington; only micropropagated material is brought in.

Many gardeners will recall the attractive displays the Hopkinsons mounted at the Chelsea Flower Shows of the mid-1980s, which gained for them the full range of RHS Award Medals including two gold medals in 1983 and 1986. Forever innovative, as good business folk need to be, their attractive annual catalogues are becoming collector's pieces and more recent price lists offer seed, including that of some wild flowers by mail order. Visitors to their nursery linger in the garden where innumerable herbs and fragrant plants are set out in both informal borders — mainly for the dramatic larger herbs — and formal beds, so that the true decorative value of herbs becomes apparent and there is much to be learnt about gardening with herbs. In 1991 new borders of silver with red and pink with white replaced previous collections of bee, cosmetic and dye plants manifesting that herb gardens are moving forward from collections of plants revered for their economic value and herbs are being grown increasingly for their individual attractiveness. The shift towards scented plants proclaimed in the Hollington Logo 'Herbs and Scented Plants' picks up the early theme stated by Eleanour Sinclair Rohde in her book *The Scented Garden* (1931) and taken up by Margaret Brownlow twenty years later in *Herbs and the Fragrant Garden*. More recently Rosemary Verey's *The Scented Garden* (1981), my own *The Fragrant Garden* (1981) and Stephen Lacey's *The Scented Garden* (1991) have appeared.

MARGARET BROWNLOW

Margaret Brownlow, always referred to by Miss Hewer as 'little Margaret', began work at The Herb Farm in 1933, and then after qualifying in horticulture at the University of Reading in 1938 returned there. The soubriquet of 'Little Margaret' summed up precisely her willingness to run about for her employer and her unassuming nature, yet from her biography one senses that her qualities were not fully appreciated generally in the herb world. Margaret Brownlow was artistic and produced simple trade catalogues with delightful 'rainbow' colours depicting a range of herbs. Her book *Herbs and the Fragrant Garden* (1957) became a Bible for a generation of herb enthusiasts and it was illustrated by her own crayon and watercolour panels and embellished by her own simple poems.

Her privately published 'memoirs' (1964) subsequent to her major book, affords a time capsule insight into herb gardens of the early 1960s. Alas, she does not record a single date! Her lists of suggested plants for gardens she was planning fail also to reveal a clue as to *when* the work was in hand.

One of the gardens she designed was at Knole Castle, Kent, Vita Sackville West's family home. On a sloping site some 50 ft (50 m) square, a circular wheel bed is at the centre, the 'spokes' of which are of santolina, and the wedges of golden marjoram, red leaved sage, rock hyssop and the upright pennyroyal. Then each corner of the garden has a broadly triangular bed abounding in taller herbs. Her accompanying quotation for plants was slightly amended, and the garden planted in 1963. The thyme lawn was never made. Nothing innovative is revealed in Margaret Brownlow's style of garden design; rather her contribution was in the abundance of plants she grew and popularized.

The herb garden at Knole, set out as a huge wheel with santolina as 'spokes', and with surrounding beds, for which Margaret Brownlow submitted the accompanying estimate.

Knole — Suggested List of Herb Plants

	£	S	D
96 Santolina incanc @ 32/- per doz	12	16	0
24 Red Sage @ 25/- per doz	2	10	0
24 Golden Marjoram @ 22/- per doz	2	4	0
24 Blue Rock Hyssop @ 22/- per doz	2	4	0
24 Upright Pennyroyal @ 27/9d per doz	2	15	6
90 Golden Thymes @ 22/- per doz	7	14	0
(All above for central wheel-bed)			
128 Silver Posie Thymes @ 22/- per doz	11	0	0
24 Hidcote Giant Lavenders @ 27/9d per doz	2	15	0
72 Seal Lavenders @ 27/9d per doz	8	0	0

120 English Yew, 2½/3 ft. high	63 – 0 – 0
8 Southernwoods	1 – 4 – 0
4 Junipers (*Juniperus communis*)	2 – 0 – 0
12 Clary Sage	2 – 5 – 0
18 Scarlet Bergamot	1 – 18 – 6
18 Purple Bergamot	1 – 18 – 6
19 Old Lady @ 22/- per dozen	1 – 14 – 0
10 "Camphor Plant"	1 – 2 – 6
12 Perennial Marjoram	1 – 2 – 0
29 Lemon Thyme 22/- doz	2 – 13 – 0
12 Blue Hyssop	1 – 2 – 0
12 Pink Hyssop	1 – 5 – 0
12 White Horehound	1 – 2 – 0
21 Wormwood	1 – 17 – 0
22 Savory	2 – 0 – 0
12 Spearmint	1 – 2 – 0
12 French Marjoram	1 – 5 – 0
9 Rue	18 – 0
6 Tarragon, True French	1 – 4 – 0
12 Various Thyme	1 – 6 – 0
9 Angelica	18 – 0
6 Alecost	15 – 0
3 Sweetbriar	15 – 0
8 Bowles Mint	16 – 0
18 Curry Plant	2 – 0 – 0
12 Chives	1 – 2 – 0
10 Lovage	1 – 2 – 6
12 Peppermint	1 – 5 – 0
8 Golden Sage	1 – 12 – 0
5 Marsh Mallow	12 – 6
12 Eau de Cologne Mint	1 – 5 – 0
9 Rosemary, 3/6d size	1 – 11 – 0
12 Mentha rubra raripila	1 – 7 – 9
10 Common Thyme	1 – 0 – 0
8 Sorrel, Bd-leaf	16 – 0
12 Fennel	1 – 2 – 0
12 Santolina Lemon Queen	1 – 7 – 9
9 Sweet Cicely	1 – 11 – 0
9 Burnet	18 – 0
12 Parsley	16 – 6
10 Variegated Apple Mint	1 – 2 – 6
8 Lemon Balm	16 – 0
	£169 – 13 – 6

Creeping Thymes for lawn:
3.240 (rate of 4 per square foot) £160
1,620 (rate of 2 per square foot) .... £ 80

E & O E

Some mints form one of the illustrations painted by the author in Herbs and the Fragrant Garden. *1 ginger mint, 2 crisped peppermint, 3 apple mint (Bowles), 4 black peppermint, 5 variegated apple mint, 6 Mentha rubra raripila, 7 round-leaved mint. 8 spearmint, 9 pennyroyal, 10 eau de Cologne mint, 11 horsemint, 12 Mentha requienii 13 Japanese mint, 14 Mentha gattefossei.*

Scented gardens

Scented gardens 'for the blind' were a popular approach in the 1960s. Margaret Brownlow lists them at Kingston Parish Church in the centre of the town; Queens Park, Harborne, Birmingham, Warwickshire; King George V Memorial Garden in Eldon Square, Reading, Berkshire; University Botanic Garden, Cambridge; Westgate Gardens, Canterbury, Kent; The Brook Scented Garden, St Anne's Garden, Hove, Sussex; Lloyd Park, Walthamstow; Wrexham, Felixstowe, Bournemouth (then) in

Hampshire; Totnes, Devon; Bexley, Kent; Yarmouth and Wisbech, Cambridgeshire and admits the list is not exhaustive. This period — late 1950s and early 1960s — witnessed the revival of the old nosegay gardens and afforded a renewed importance to fragrant plants. Not everything grown in such gardens were herbs; lilac (*Syringa vulgaris*), mock orange (*Philadelphus coronaria*), H T roses, and wallflowers (*Cheiranthus cheiri*), for example, were also grown, but the majority of plants were those rich in essential oils. However, in looking at a wider range of plants than aromatic herbs for the scented garden, Margaret Brownlow set herbs first. Thus plants like costmary, sweet Cicely and lovage which in the early 1930s Miss Rohde had complained were unobtainable, had in the intervening years been retrieved and much of the credit goes to work done at The Herb Farm and early herb nurseries.

It becomes evident when we indulge in retrospect over the activities at Seal, and the work of Eleanour Sinclair Rohde and by Margaret Brownlow after the War, that the South Eastern region of England was where the present vogue for herb gardening had its inception. The counties of Kent and Sussex constituted the hub of activity perhaps because of the belief in a supportive dry warm climate. (Subsequently popularity has shown that the damper warmth of the western counties and the Welsh border lands are admirably suited to herbs, and indeed the crisp air of East Anglia.) Rather the burgeoning was inspired and nurtured by a group of women in that part of the country. Gertrude Jekyll in Surrey had found the key to a gardening style, and while her own herb garden designs were sparse and shunned, the mode was engagingly expressed by herb plants. Ada Teetgen who elucidated contradictory written material on the subject of herbs lived at Orpington, Kent, as did Dorothy Hewer and Margaret Brownlow, who did so much to popularize the words 'Herb Farm'. It was in the garden behind her home Cranham Lodge, Reigate that Eleanour Sinclair Rohde first experimented with herb growing and unusual vegetables. About 1946 she designed a herb garden at Lullingstone Castle, Kent as part of a commercial project with Heath & Heather. Based on the monastic garden plan where individual herbs were each allotted a single rectangular bed, the 'pave and plant' idea was used where 'silver santolina, golden thyme, mauve catmint and purple bergamots desported themselves around a central bed of old roses'. Alas, the garden was modified after her death, following some of the plans she had formulated in the 1930s.

Above left: *The (undated) catalogue cover for The Herb Farm at Seal, painted by Margaret Brownlow illustrates the wide range of aromatic plants she cultivated. They include several pelargoniums,* Teucrium fruitcans, Perowski atriplicifolia, Myrtus communis, Rubus odoratum, *rue,* Caryopteris clandonensis *and* Brittonastrum mexicanum *(Syn.* Agastache mexicanum*).*

Above right: *Poisonous drug plants painted by Margaret Brownlow include 1 woody nightshade, 2 wood spurge, 3 green hellebore, 4 hemlock, 5 monkshood, 6 henbane, 7 foxglove, 8 thornapple, 9 black nightshade, 10 opium lettuce, 11 opium poppy, 12 belladonna, 13 bryony, 14 fritillary, 15 colchicum, 16 spurge laurel, 17 pulsatilla, 18 mandrake.*

A BOOK ON HERBALS AND THE INFLUENCE OF STYLE

Into the calm waters of the horticultural and botanical world of 1912 had come an account of printed herbals from the fifteenth to the seventeenth centuries. The majority were European but as Agnes Arber the author explained they had given her so much pleasure that she hoped others may derive enjoyment in reading about them. Her interest was aroused at the early age of 15 years when she knew already that she wished to be a botanist, she examined a copy of Henry Lyte's *A Niewe Herball* (1578) and drawing upon her cultured background and her study of botanical history she published in 1912 *Herbals, Their Origin and Evolution*. (The book has remained a classic, and was updated in 1938 and again in 1953 and was produced facsimile in U.S.A. in 1970.) As a research botanist and philosopher Agnes Arber (née Robertson) continued to publish a stream of scientific papers and philosphical books up to 1959. She died at Cambridge in 1960 in her 82nd year. It is sad to reflect that because her book aroused an interest in herbals among the bibliophiles, it put the prices far beyond her modest means and prevented her from assembling her own collection.

ELEANOUR SINCLAIR ROHDE

One person who was irrevocably influenced by *Herbals* was the young intellectual Eleanour Sinclair Rohde. This willowy girl had been educated at Cheltenham Ladies College and St. Hilda's Oxford and had spent three years as Secretary to Lord Curzon at Kedlestone, Yorkshire. There is little doubt that her interest in garden history and traditional plants stemmed from the research she did during the ten years following Agnes Arber's book.

She devoted hours to studying English MS herbals, both in person and by correspondence with the librarians at cathedrals and private library owners. She visited the British Museum and travelled to Cambridge to work in the library at Trinity College and Jesus College and at Oxford conversed with librarians at most of the Oxford Colleges and worked in the Bodleian library which she had known in her student days. Her primary interest was the MS herbal of the tenth to fourteenth centuries and contemporary treatise on the virtues of herbs. Whereas Agnes Arber had concentrated on printed herbals, Eleanour Sinclair Rohde enlarged up English works and was able to provide a catalogue of early MSS and their whereabouts as an Appendix to *The Old English Herbals* (1922). Two years later came *Old English Garden Books* and a flow of articles for *Country Life, The Queen, The Sphere, The Field* and later the *Journal of the Royal Horticultural Society* on a range of garden and plant related subjects. A first book however in 1920 was entitled *A Garden of Herbs*.

Meanwhile at her home in Reigate, having lost her brother during 1916, she looked after her parents and experimented with herbs and other traditional plants. Her horticultural interests appear to have shied away from the highly decorative and been concentrated on economic plants and old plants. She was at least interested in, if not in fact cultivating, herbs by 1918 because circumstantial evidence suggests that she became a member of The British Guild of Herb Growers.

During the 1920s more books followed and in the 1930s came a volley of books on herbs and herb gardening. By this time she did much of her work in the library of Nyman's Sussex, home of her friends Lt. Col. L. C. R. and Mrs Messel. Alas, her MSS and papers are believed to have perished in the fire there; others were bequeathed to a younger cousin. Col. Messel and his gardener Mr J. Comber gave advice on plants, as did the Hon. Vicary Gibbs who had a remarkable garden at Aldenham House, Hertfordshire, and there is little doubt that these friends influenced her attachment to old bush roses, and the ways in which roses had been employed in domestic recipes in the past, inspiring her delightful book *Rose Recipes from Olden Times* (1939). During the early 1930s she wrote two books, *The Scented Garden* (1931) in which she acknowledged help from The Hon. Vicary Gibbs and Mr Comber and *The Story of the Garden* (1934). In this one of her American friends collaborated and contributed the chapter on American Gardens. Louisa King, a notable garden writer in America, who lived in Alma, Michigan had over many years corresponded with and collaborated with writers and editors on both sides of the Atlantic. She and Miss Jekyll corresponded, and Louisa King visited England in January, 1914, not to visit gardens but to attend a Women's Conference. Eleanour Sinclair Rohde's work was acclaimed and appreciated in America and it was only after the War that she was able to go there on a six-week lecture tour.

In turn her writing, particularly that on the subject of herbs appealed to gardeners, especially to lady gardeners. A market was being created for 'luxury herbs' during the late 1920s and 1930s by such people as Edith Hughes, Dorothy Hewer and Hilda Leyel at their shops, none of whom manifest Eleanour Sinclair Rohde's background understanding of the traditional value of herbs or herb products as scented conceits.

While their interests centred up the growing of medicinal herbs in the case of Miss Hewer and herbal medicine for Mrs Leyel — although the two ladies never saw eye to eye — Miss Rohde created ideals by her writing, which appealed to gardeners. A herb garden she said 'conjures up a vision, as remote and yet as familiar as memory, of a scheduled pleasaunce full of sunlight and delicious scents and radiant with colours and quiet charm of all the lovable old-fashioned plants one so rarely sees nowadays'.

She did not live in isolation, and moreover had passed her formative years absorbing some of the influences of the Arts and Crafts Movement and of Robinson and Jekyllian natural planting ideas. Devoted as she was to all things past — in fact she 'lived' in the past, never quite accepting the loss of her brother who had been reported 'missing' in 1916 — her gardening schemes were uninfluenced by the modern gardens of the 1930s and related closely to medieval plots where herbs could be related to their spiritual and symbolic backdrop, as her earliest plans reveal. Her high significance in the twentieth century development of decorative herb gardens is unquestioned.

An intricate design for a bee garden, drawn by Margaret Oden for Eleanour Sinclair Rohde's 1943 catalogue. It became familiar as the catalogue cover for Kathleen Hunter who took over some of Miss Sinclair Rohde's stock and continued work with unusual vegetables.

DEVELOPING A GARDEN STYLE

Two of a set of twelve postcards designed by Eleanour Sinclair Rohde and painted by Hilda Coley were published in the 1930s by the Medici Society. Each shows two selected herbs and a short note about their values.

The magic of Edwardian gardening fractured with the outbreak of the 1914–18 War. But as the threads in the story of plants were taken up again, the over-the-shoulder backward glance was still apparent. Old world gardens still claimed their appeal.

By 1920 a garden was being made at New Place, Stratford-upon-Avon replacing a mid-Victorian one, in an Elizabethan (or Shakespearean) style. It is still maintained today, and although slightly adapted in content many of the plants are herbs. Nearby in the same town at Hall's Croft, the home of Shakespeare's daughter and son-in-law, Dr John Hall, physician and apothecary, there is a garden with old world plants some of them herbs. Indoors an Elizabethan dispensary has been reconstructed. It was in his practice that Dr Hall discovered the value of some fresh herbs in the relief of scurvy.

Surprisingly, few references remain to herb gardens made following the War but one lengthy account of a garden started *c.* 1920 is that of Lady Margaret Watney at Cornbury Park, Oxfordshire. It was situated in the nut garden, one of the walled gardens created there in the seventeenth century by John Evelyn for Lord Clarendon. Cornbury had been granted to Lord Clarendon by Charles II at the time of the restoration, but a previous ranger had been Lord Henry Danby the founder of the Oxford Botanic Garden. Lord Clarendon himself while in exile in France had written to his daughter-in-law 'Speake to thy husbande that when he finds the opportunity of any friends cominge this way, he will send me Gerard's Herball'.

The garden Lady Margaret made formed a long south-facing border 10–12 ft (3–3.6 m) deep and arranged in the pattern of herbaceous border planting; taller plants at the back, smaller ones at the front. Herbs were collected mainly from the wild to form this border and an elderly gardener relates how repeated efforts to establish eyebright failed until a block of turf upon which it was growing was introduced. Lady Margaret compiled a delightful little book listing 103 herbs she grew in her border. She remarked in the preface '. . , there is no need to have the dingy border we are apt to associate with the words "Herb Garden"'.

Early decorative herb gardens

Eleanour Sinclair Rohde studied garden history and old herbals and did much to enhance the quality and range of herbs in cultivation. Her imaginative genius conceived the rectangular enclosed herb garden on a level site. Miss Rohde drew her garden plans on linen and explained the planting details. The earliest plan to survive shows chamomile and thyme paths and each bed is outlined by an evergreen plant. 'To make an effective Herb Garden' she wrote, 'the general design should, I think, be laid out chiefly with evergreen or nearly evergreen herbs'. She used 32 herbs, mirrored in design in each half of the garden on a plot 90 ft × 60 ft (27 m × 18 m). She promoted the philosophy that although a herb garden may be enriched with flowers it should be primarily a green garden.

A second plan to survive, also portrays a rectangular plot which she described as having stately herbs in the outer beds, herbs 'of middle growth' in the inner beds and in the centre a knot of marigolds and thyme. Both plans portray golden marigolds to catch the eye as a central feature. Plants treasured and described by Turner, Gerard, Parkinson and Culpeper, plants written about with erudition by Lindley and Mrs Grieve were brought to recogition in a novel way.

Unobtrusive gardens

That herb gardens were made in the 1920s and 1930s is certain, but remarkably inadequate descriptions remain. Garden literature and gardening journals did not record herb gardens. Garden brochures for visitors were souvenirs to be devised by future commercially minded managers; thus the dearth of fact leaves a void in the story. I recall clearly visiting what seemed to be a sizeable herb garden at Bray, Berkshire close to the bank of the river Thames during the War, about the summer of 1941. As so often in youth, we do not realize the significance of an event at the time. I understand now that it must have been an early example of a formal herb garden. Skep-style bee hives formed the central feature and plants I had seen before only as wild flowers, tumbled about the borders. The owner propounded the theories of astrological botany, her sowing and harvesting directed by the Moon's phase, and indoors trestle tables carried boxes and trays of richly fragrant drying herbs.

Sissinghurst Castle

When Vita (Victoria) Sackville West and her husband Harold Nicholson bought Sissinghurst Castle, Kent in 1930, they set about restoring the property and developing a garden. He planned the skeleton of a series of enclosed small gardens, she master-minding the planting. A surrounding yew hedge was planted in the winter of 1937–38 to shelter a small square plot as a herb garden, well away from the house. (As Jane Brown has pointed out in *Vita's Other World*, the mistress of this herb garden was no cook.) The little garden which was destined to capture legendary importance, held no more than a dozen herbs beneath the skies in which battles raged for the next few years. By the mid-1940s it had become a potato patch in an effort to clear the ground from its entanglement of neglect. In 1947–48 the herb garden was relaid and extended as a quartered plot, each bed divided further by grass paths. Transformed, with a shallow stone basin planted with thymes as a central feature, it held the magic of a Paradise garden to be enjoyed in a contemplative way from a convenient stone bench, bearded by *Mentha requienii*.

Whereas Eleanour Sinclair Rohde had emphasized a central bed much in the tradition of a parterre, at Sissinghurst the central feature, although not Medieval-style water, re-established the layout of pre-Christian gardens of the Ancient World and those of Medieval Europe including England. We have seen that such compact arrangements of formal beds fitted snugly into cloister garths and developed into elaborate knots in the Elizabethan days. By then the Medieval central conduit had been transformed as a fountain, and today in some gardens is represented by a bird bath.

Writing about herb gardens in 1955 Vita Sackville West made the point 'I think a herb garden ought to be quite separate all on its own'. She had had time to consider the aesthetic value of a herb garden having made a small one first at Long Barn, her

previous home. While there is no evidence that she met or corresponded with Eleanour Sinclair Rohde, undoubtedly she was influenced by her writing and her ideas. The plants she selected for the Sissinghurst herb garden portrayed a bounty of silver foliage, peaceful pinks and bee-enticing herbs.

Nor be the little space forgot
For herbs to spice the kitchen pot;
Mint, pennyroyal, bergamot
Tarragon and melilot,
Dill for witchcraft, prisoner's rue,
Coriander, costmary,
Tansy, thyme, sweet Cicely
Saffron, balm and rosemary
That since the Virgin threw her cloak
Across it, so say country folk
Has changed its flowers from white to blue.

Vita Sackville West, The Land

Herbs in the garden at Sissinghurst in May 1948

caraway	yellow allium
melilot	silver thyme
burnet	camphor
clary	hyssop
elecampane	pink hyssop
costmary	vervain
marjoram	balm
woad	mullein
borage	bronze fennel
Anchusa 'Dropmore Opal'	dill
lemon mint	horehound
apple mint	bush basil
eau de Cologne mint	purslane
black peppermint	coriander
white peppermint	pennyroyal
herba barona	wormwood
lovage	*Bergamot* 'Cambridge Scarlet'
giant chive	*Bergamot* 'Rose Queen'
garlic	*Bergamot* 'Rare Pink'
calamint	tansy
Iris florentina (orris root)	catmint
fennel	angelica
Artemisia maritima (old lady)	*Artemisia abrotanum* (old man)
santolina	coriander
lemon thyme	Balkan sage
winter savory	sorrel
good King Henry	comfrey
germander	marigold
musk mallow	

By 1967 the National Trust had taken control of the garden at Sissinghurst and the gentle turved paths of the herb garden had to be replaced by drained stout and durable paving to withstand the feet of the constant flow of pilgrims who flock to that spot. Now it is one of the most visited, most photographed and best known herb gardens in the UK. Ask about it and few visitors can recall the plants they have seen there — substantial evidence of its atmospheric appeal!

INFLUENCE OF SISSINGHURST

The proliferation and development in style in herb gardens that followed throughout the 25 years from the remaking of Vita Sackville West's initiatory example at Sissinghurst reflected an increased understanding and respect for herbs. Fired by the developing holistic lifestyle on the one hand and an over-riding preoccupation with period gardening on the other the herbs came into their own as garden favourites.

Margaret Brownlow, working at The Herb Farm, Seal in Kent, had done much to popularize conserve and cultivate herbs. In her memoirs *The Delights of Herb Growing* (1964) she records several herb gardens of the late 1950s and early 1960s including those at Gravetye Manor, Sussex, the former home of William Robinson; and at The Red House Museum, Christchurch, Hants/Dorset, where there was a remarkable collection of herbs and wild plants at that time, many of which are still cultivated there. Another she described was at Scotney Castle, home of the late Christopher Hussey, constructed on sloping ground at East Grinstead Plastic Surgery Hospital where Dr Macindoe had worked during and after the War.

The National Trust took the initiative in the 1970s in making good decorative herb gardens at some of their properties — although by today's standards one or two of the earlier ones class as simple parterres — and then the Royal Horticultural Society followed in the late 1970s.

The Wisley herb garden

In the RHS garden at Wisley, the herb garden was deliberately designed to categorize plants for presentation — medicinal, dye, culinary, American or economic. It replaced a small border of mixed herbs elsewhere at Wisley and on a fresh site of 30-yards (27.5 m) square its inception made an important statement in 1978, proclaiming that the formal herb garden was in fashion. The original design of the herb garden at Wisley was carried out by David Palmer, then Technical Assistant to the Director. Thirty or so beds include a comprehensive range of herbs and their decorative forms lavishly planted with less common plants (at that time) such as false indigo (*Baptisia tinctoria*), plain-leaved parsley (*Petroselinum crispum*), Russian comfrey (*Symphytum peregrinum*), *Monarda citriodora* and *Serratula tinctora*. If nothing more, the completion of the herb garden at Wisley confirmed to all visitors the intuitive realization that (at last!) herbs should be taken seriously.

Plants in the Herb Garden at Wisley 1984

Bed 1
Allium schoenoprasum
Salvia officinalis 'Woodcote Farm'
Thymus vulgaris 'Rotundifolia'
Mentha spicata
Origanum vulgare
Rumex scutatus
Papaver 'Hungarian Blue Birdseed'

Bed 2
Buxus sempervirens 'Suffruticosa'
Thymus nitidus
Allium fistulosum
Origanum vulgare
Thymus No. 6
Salvia officinalis (narrow-leaved form)

Bed 3
Allium schoenoprasum
Foeniculum vulgare ssp.
    piperitum
Levisticum officinalis
Rumex acetosa
Cichorium intybus
Mellisa officinalis
Thymus vulgaris 'Lemon Curd'

Bed 4
Satureia hortensis
Achillea decolorans
Origanum vulgare var
    prismaticum
Mentha spicata 'Lacerata'
Sanguisorba minor
Origanum heracleoticum
Thymus herba-barona
Origanum tyttanthum
Rosmarinus officinalis
Ocimum basilicum 'Dark
    Opel'
Thymus vulgaris 'Annie Hall'
Thymus vulgaris 'E B
    Anderson'

Bed 5
Chamaemelum nobile fl.pl.

Bed 6
Pimpinella anisum
Mentha spicata var *latifolia*
Thymus vulgaris

Bed 7 _(preceded by list)_
Allium scorodoprasum
Mentha suaveolens
Thymus vulgaris 'Aureus'
Salvia officinalis
Origanum vulgare 'Webb's
    White'
Allium cepa 'Perutile'
Thymus No. 3
Carum carvi
Thymus nummularius
Coriandrum sativum
Allium fistulosum
Sium sisarum

Bed 7
Mentha longifolia
Myrrhis odorata
Salvia officinalis (narrow-
    leaved form)
Foeniculum officinale
Armoracia rusticana
Origanum vulgare 'Aureum
    Variegatum'
Tanacetum vulgare

Bed 8
Origanum sp.
Thymus sp.
Origanum creticum
Buxus sempervirens
    'Suffruticosa'
Symphytum officinalis
Foeniculum officinalis

Bed 9
Anethum graveolens
Chenopodium bonus-henricus
Salvia officinalis (Spanish
    form)
Angelica archangelica
Morus nigra
Mentha × villosa
Artemisia dracunculus

Bed 10
Phytolacca esculenta
Anthemis tinctoria 'Wargrave'
Serratula tinctoria
Isatis tinctoria
Baptisia tinctoria
Rhamnus infectoria
Calendula officinalis
Asperula tinctoria
Dicra occidentale

Bed 11
Genista tinctoria
Coreopsis tinctoria
Asperula tinctoria
Isatis tinctoria
Portulacca oleracea

The herb garden at Sissinghurst Castle, Kent in 1975 by which time the paved paths had replaced the original turf to accommodate the innumerable visitors.

Work in progress 1978 at the Royal Horticultural Society's garden, Wisley, Surrey where an extensive herb garden was being made.

The finished garden has provided both pleasure and instruction to many visitors and in consequence the quiet fragrant atmosphere of a herb garden seems to have been lacking.

Bed 12
Delphinium semibarbatum
Serratula tinctoria
Asperula tinctoria
Anchusa (hybrids)
Thymus vulgaris 'Doone Valley'
Borago officinalis
Isatis tinctoria

Bed 13
Vinca minor 'Variegata'
Salvia officinalis
Hyoscyamus albus
Myrtus communis

Bed 14
Thymus vulgaris
Viola odorata
Verbena officinalis
Thymus citriodorus 'Silver Posie'
Reseda luteola
Ocimum basilicum

Bed 15
Opoanax chironium
Chrysanthemum coccineum
Saponaria officinalis
Apocynum cannabinum
Salvia officinalis (white-flowered form)
Chrysanthemum cinerariifolium
Althaea cannabina
Hibiscus cannabinus

Bed 16
Lavandula angustifolia
Ruta graveolens 'Jackman's Blue'
Foeniculum vulgare (bronze form)
Glycyrrhiza glabra
Harniaria glabra
Hesperis matronalis
Papaver somnifera
Carum carvi

Bed 17
Buxus sempervirens 'Suffruticosa'
Rosa gallica 'Marcel Bourhouin'
Polygonum bistorta 'Superbum'
Cedronella canariensis
Valeriana officinalis

Bed 18
Gentian lutea
Melissa officinalis
Chrysanthemum balsamita
Rosa gallica 'Officinalis'
Marrubium vulgare
Hyssopus officinalis
Scutelaria laterifolia

Bed 19
Salvia sclarea
Papaver somniferum plena

Teucrium maru
Ruta chalepensis
Mentha pulegium
Rosa gallica 'Antonia D'Ormois'
Valeriana officinalis ssp. *officinalis*
Santolina rosmarinifolia
Salvia carviflorum
Clandula officinalis

Bed 20
Chamaemelum nobile 'Treneague'

Bed 21
Mentha pulegium
Santolina chamaecyparissus
Lavandula angustifolia
Chrysanthemum parthenium
Artemisia pontica
Lavandula stoechas
Mentha gentilis 'Variegata'

Bed 22
Buxus sempervirens 'Suffruticosa'
Paeonia officinalis
Glycyrrhiza echinata
Rheum officinale

Bed 23
Symphytum peregrinum
Ruta graveolens 'Variegata'
Digitalis montana
Inule helenium

Bed 24
Tanacetum vulgare 'Crispum'
Mentha × piperita
Artemisia absinthium 'Lambrook Silver'
Galega officinalis
Althaea officinalis
Ajuga reptans
Mentha longifolia
Pulmonaria officinalis

Bed 25
Chrysanthemum balsamita 'Tomentosa'
Lavandula 'Hidcote Giant'
Monarda fistulosa
Salvia officinalis 'Icterina'
Hyssopus officinalis ssp. *aristatus*
Rosa damascena 'Conte de Chambord'
Galium odoratum
Salvia uliginosa
Thymus 'Porlock'

Bed 26
Nepeta camphorata
Salvia lavandulifolia
Thymus 'Winter Gold'
Thymus sp.
Thymus hirsutus
Salvia officinalis
Chrysanthemum parthenium
Lavandula latifolia

Bed 27
Artemisia camphorata
Mentha × piperita 'Citrata'
Ifis florentina
Monarda citriodora
Symphytum sp.

Bed 28
Salvia officinalis 'Tricolor'
Lavandula burmanii
Salvia transcaucasica
Hyssopus officinalis (pink-flowered form)
Mentha suaveolens 'Variegata'
Micromeria thymifolia
Origanum vulgare 'Aureum'
Thymus praecox ssp. *polytrichus*

Bed 29
Hyssopus officinalis ssp. *aristatus*
Lavandula angustifolia
Thymus 'Boothmans Var.'
Chrysanthemum parthenium 'Bowles Double'
Micromeria piperella
Thymus 'Porlock'
Pycnanthemum flexuosum
Thymus vulgaris 'Silver Posie'
Rosmarinus officinalis ssp. *corsicus* 'Prostratus'

Bed 30
Lippia citriodora
Mentha villosa 'Alopecuroides'
Artemisia douglasiana
Rosmarinus officinalis 'Primley Blue'
Ocimum basilicum 'Dark Opel'
Hyssopus officinalis (white-flowered form)

Bed 31
Rosa centifolia 'Ombree Parfaite'
Artemisia dracunculus
Helichrysum angustifolium
Nepeta mussini
Calamintha nepetoides
Monarda clinopodia
Lavandula 'Jean Davis'
Monarda punctata
Mentha asiatica
Monarda didyma 'Croftway Pink'
Nepeta mussini
Origanum vulgare 'Aureum'
Artemisia procera
Lavandula 'Alriel'
Origanum virens
Hyssopus sp.
Lavandula 'Mailette'

Surrounding hedge:
Rosmarinus officinalis 'Miss Jessop's Upright'

VII

HERB GARDENS TODAY

PRESENT DAY HERB GARDENS

While clearly there is a collective consciousness about herb garden design, those created during the latter half of the present century display a range of creative ideas. Nevertheless, they fall into two main categories, the informal and the formal. Undoubtedly the informal relates to the cottage garden border, when herbs were grown cheek by jowl, probably for practical reasons, with the tallest, such as angelica and lovage at the back.

Informal herb gardens

Some informal herb gardens are merely a border of herbs backed by a wall or hedge as for the conventional herbaceous border. The impact then depends upon the dimension and season. Others are island-bed open borders such as the herb garden at *Harlow Carr*, The Northern Horticultural Society's garden at Harrogate, North Yorkshire. Money was donated for a herb garden in 1982, the site and open border style suggested by Pippa Rakhusen. Replanted in 1987 in the same style, it allows inspection freely. Borders of this kind represent the oldest and the simplest form of categorizing plants. Others adopt the 'pave and plant' idea where individual paving stones are set in a chequer-board fashion, each intervening bed being filled with one sort of herb. Here is a direct reference to the Medieval idea of 'one bed one plant'. Such treatment allows ideally for an informal area of a garden to be treated formally, or extended as time and resources allow. An example is to be seen at the *Birmingham Botanic Garden*, Edgbaston, Birmingham, and at *Lackham College of Agriculture*, near Chippenham, Wiltshire. At *Stoke Park*, Northamptonshire, the pave-and-plant theme was used superbly on two levels to produce the most impressively delightful herb garden ever designed by the head gardener.

Hefty borders of herbs are undoubtedly at their best at *Acorn Bank*, Temple Sowerby, Cumbria, where the National Trust established a herb garden, initially of physic plants, more than twenty years ago in 1969. Within the old kitchen garden, the brick walls of which provide protection from the bitter Helm wind from the east, herbs are grouped lavishly in the style of a conventional herbaceous or cottage border. A seventeenth-century lead water tank is now filled with cushions of thyme, bearberry and germander. Nearby a tiny bog herb garden sits outside a greenhouse in which scented-leaved plants are housed.

At *Threave* near Castle Douglas, Scotland, where young gardeners are trained by The National Trust for Scotland, herbs are planted in an impressive border backed by a wall. Partly decorative and partly practical arcs of paving stone extend from the wall base to the path edge to facilitate maintenance of the plants in the border. Elsewhere randomly placed stepping stones meander among a collection of mints, each cunningly restrained from wandering (as mint is wont to do) by brick guards.

Similar bold beds and borders form the herb garden at *Cranborne Manor*, Dorset, and in several private gardens. It is to the latter locations that some of the prettiest herb collections are made, many of them in borders and beds informally disposed. *Gaulden Manor*, near Taunton, Somerset is one such, where the herb garden is set in the form of a cross, with sundial at the centre to mark the timelessness of herbs. Well-placed portable containers ensure that there is always something to enjoy in the herb garden there. Another delightful private garden is set in the fold of the house at *Deans Court*, Wimborne, Dorset, where Lady Hanham has set her herbs in gravel. The gravel mulch idea was used for herbs and foliage plants at *Denmans*, Sussex, by Mrs Robinson before John Brookes designed the present herb garden.

Am impressive herb garden at Stoke Park, Northamptonshire was made by Gilbert Cook the head gardener. It echoes the Medieval chequerboard design, now called pave-and-plant, on two levels. The scheme breaks away from the traditional central feature, with classical urns at each corner.

Informality is continued as a theme in chamomile lawns and pathways that emit a delightful fruity fragrance when underfoot. At the *University of Leicester Botanic Garden*, the main area of the Southmeade herb garden displays an extensive thyme lawn which unrolls as a pink and silver carpet in summer. A thyme lawn, in a paved setting is a minor attraction of *Sissinghurst Castle*, Kent.

Formal herbal gardens

By far the most popular designs display formality, indeed so rigid that it has come to be accepted that these humble plants, perhaps ineffective for garden decoration in themselves, require the support of a designed presentation, even one that makes a statement. Garden guides and brochures entice visitors with the words 'traditional herb garden', which more precisely should read 'garden of traditional herbs'. Almost universally the design belies historical reference. Before the eighteenth century when the sweeping landscape begged curves and slopes, all gardens in England were formal, although the word was not applied. Without question it is pertinent to set herbs into such a context and most herb gardens made during the past two decades are in this style.

To assemble plants of a Tudor association in a knot garden seems justifiably representative of the period. But when in the seventeenth and eighteenth centuries the knot designs were developed and extended as parterres, the herbs were gradually banished, superseded for decoration by the exotic newcomers. Herbs as economic, culinary or physic plants were besported in the kitchen garden, as Batty Langley decreed, and so were never part of the picture in the developing decorative styles of layout. It is not difficult therefore to accept that the twentieth-century proliferation of formal herb gardens not only proclaims a renewed recognition of many traditional plants, but is a contemporary product. The moorings of modern garden style — herbaceous planting, woodland gardens and adaptations of the romantic cottage garden — are a hundred years old, and rely upon the concepts of Robinson and Jekyll. The emergence of the formal herb garden is contemporary with much of that, but has had to wait for the post-war holistic life style to sponsor it. Now, it can be said with considerable conviction that the formal herb garden is the principal innovation in garden style that posterity will inherit from the latter half of the twentieth century. Thus it is the plants themselves that linger over the centuries entwining various periods of garden history with a repetitive theme. Old sources are resuscitated in so many guises.

Many modern formal presentations depend upon a theme, assembling Bible herbs, culinary herbs, dye plants, pot pourri plants, medicinal, household, Shakespeare,

Above: *In 1969 the National Trust converted the old kitchen garden at Acorn Bank, Cumbria into a garden for medicinal plants. The collection now exceeds 190 different kinds.*

Left: *In many private gardens a corner set aside for herbs offers an air of timelessness and retreat. One such was the small herb garden during the 1980s at Gaulden Manor, Somerset. (Photograph 1981)*

Chaucer or monastic association. We are left wondering why herbs have to be collected according to whim. It is not the juxtaposition of plants for garden effect that Miss Jekyll advocated, but an attempt to categorize in much the same way that a botanic garden sets out the Natural Order beds (never to be despised for many herbs lurk there among their relatives).

One small formal herb garden of note and its nearby border emphasizes dye plants. Designed by Ian Mylles in 1964, the herb garden at *The American Museum in Britain*, Claverton Manor, Bath, Avon, was one of the first to include dye plants as a justifiable category of herbs. Indigo, pokeroot, alkanet and woad are included and other plants that the American settlers employed for dyeing home-woven cloth. A traditional beehive (devoid of bees!) sits at the centre of the diminutive and charming herb plot. Present-day large herb gardens, with the exception of Acorn Bank can be described as formal in design as at *Cranborne Manor*, Dorset; *Hatfield House*, Hertfordshire; *Chenies Manor*, Hertfordshire, The Royal Horticultural Society's garden at *Wisley*, Surrey and *The Queen's Garden* at the Royal Botanic Gardens, Kew are all described elsewhere.

Historical sites

Quite rightly, innumerable newly-made gardens on historical sites, or those related to buildings of historical importance are herb gardens. The preoccupation with the past for both garden designers and restorers has supported a widening interest in cultivating herbs; colloquially it is called 'gardening in period'.

One of the paramount examples of such a garden is that made behind *The Tudor House Museum*, Southampton and opened in July 1982, overlooking Southampton Water. In an area about 30 yards (27.5 m) square a Tudor garden has been created where not only are all the plants herbs, but many features of the period are displayed: the chamomile seat, the carpenter's work, the royal beasts and the central knot with its encompassing elm railing. Dr Sylvia Landsberg researched and laid out this garden along the instructions given by the sixteenth-century writer William Lawson in *The Countrie Huswife's Garden* and the central knot design was taken from *The Gardener's Labyrinth* by Didymus Mountaine (this being the *nom de plume* of Thomas Hyll.) Thus a garden of plants known in Tudor times forms an intriguing garden of today. Labels proclaim the vernacular name and scientific name, provenance of the plant and when it was first recorded.

Another period garden designed by Dr Landsberg for the Hampshire Gardens Trust is *Queen Eleanor's Garden* behind the Great Hall at Winchester. While many of the plants included there are herbs, the distinction is emphasized between a period garden and a herb garden. Features of a supposed garden of the thirteenth century have been created — stone benches, a tunnel arbour, a wall turf seat and water channels. Each plant was a herb at that time.

In the north-eastern corner of the *Chelsea Physic Garden*, in the heart of London, there is a herb garden on a site where healing herbs or physic plants have been grown since the Society of Apothecaries laid out their garden there in 1673. Originally the garden was intended as a physic garden but, as botanical and medical history was to prove, it became the hub of plant exchange and plant collecting while never relinquishing its role as a garden for the study of medical plant research. Today in conjunction with the Imperial College of Science, work continues on the value of feverfew related to the relief of migraine, and rose periwinkle (*Carthamnus rosea*) in the treatment of leukaemia. In the herb garden proper plants are collected according to their uses or association, a homoeophatic collection, plants for perfumery and dye plants.

As with many other gardens where herbs are collected according to the way in which they were employed by our forefathers, it becomes an informative garden. Watch any garden visitors and when they come to the herb beds they will examine plant by plant, recognizing them as individuals far more than when enjoying the herbaceous and shrub borders. Here they are looking for garden effect. This offers another clue as to why herb gardens are more pleasing visually when set out on geometric lines. Individual beds allow associated collections of herbs to be made.

Sites of Medieval origin on which herbs would have been cultivated have in some instances been turned into delightful herb gardens during the past two decades. At

Westminster Abbey, where there is one of the oldest known garden sites in London, a small herb border has been planted. It is judged to overlie the Abbey's Infirmary garden and, moreover, all the plants were donated by members of The British Herb Traders' Association, and put in place by their donors in a little planting ceremony in 1981. Later, when in summer fullness, the garden was blessed by The Bishop of Westminster. At the *cathedrals of Worcester, Wells* (with its William Turner association from Tudor days), *Lincoln* and *Peterborough*, pretty herb gardens gently remind the visitor of links with the past. At *Usk*, South Glamorgan, Rosie Humphreys has made a little garden of herbs with Medieval pedigree within the Castle walls. To one side an alcove enfolds a seat where garden visitors can rest to absorb the sweet-scented memories. Rosemary, lavender and roses predominate, paths are edged with fragrant pinks and thyme and about fifty other herbs, cultivated before 1596 (when Gerard was writing his herbal) are collected, ranging through aromatic, culinary and medicinal plants.

Set among the impressive ruins of *Beaulieu Abbey* in Hampshire, herbs have been planted around the sides of the old cloisters where in the past the cloister garden or 'garth' would have been. Designed by Moira Burnett in the late 1970s, herbs are set to fall like a gown at the foot of each arch, and carefully selected according to aspect to give a decorative effect rarely achieved successfully by herbs. Enhanced by square paving stones set diagonally the plants form mounds that flow outward over the pathway. A similar planting idea has been adopted at *Lincoln Cathedral* in the Cloister Garden where herbs and other plants surround the base of each pillar of Sir Christopher Wren's arcaded walk. As the cathedral is dedicated to the Blessed Virgin, each plant included has some Marian association such as we have seen enjoyed as a cult in Medieval gardens. The lovely rosemary proclaims its honour in having had the Virgin's blue cloak thrown over it while she rested, and turning its former white flowers to dusty blue.

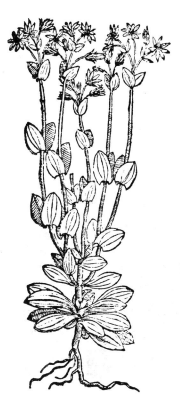

One of the first projects of the Sussex Historic Gardens Restoration Society (now the County Gardens Trust) was to establish a physic garden at the old monastic site of *Michelham Priory* near Hailsham just a few miles from Eastbourne. A site surrounded by an old moat was transformed in 1981 by Virginia Hinzen, to display about ten beds depicting medicinal plants for various ailments. In the past most plants were believed to combat a range of ailments, and the selection offered in this garden were decided upon after thorough research. Thus we find herbs for gout and rheumatism in one bed, for depression and dreams in another, for digestive disorders, for stings and bites, herbs for treating wounds and broken bones and those recommended for pulmonary and blood deficiencies. Intriguing blue enamel labels acompany the beds depicting monks preparing herbs, lest in our entrancement in the garden we overlook the medieval association. Labels of mixed quality are to be seen in many present-day herb gardens, informative and unmemorable, but the blue ones at Michelham Priory are outstandingly attractive.

Another important example of a formal garden of plants set in period is that created by The Marchioness of Salisbury at her home, *Hatfield House* in Hertfordshire. The house itself and surrounding gardens were laid out in Jacobean days, elaborately styled by John Tradescant, Saloman de Caux and Mountain Jennings. A large knot garden, set on a sunken plot before the former house, now called the Old Palace, was laid out around 1980 and abounds in sweet-scented plants grown in Tudor and Stuart times. Looking down on to the pattern, the site is quartered by brick paths, each quarter again bisected, and all the edges are trim with clipped box. Perhaps now the largest knot garden in the UK, it is a recent creation and yet perfectly complements the soft red Tudor brick of the Old Palace at one side.

Elsewhere in the garden at Hatfield Lady Salisbury has laid out a deliciously scented herb garden with chamomile path edged with paving stones to form a truly fragrant walk across the garden. Here old bush roses including *Rosa gallica* the apothecary's rose, pinks, artemisias, marjorams, lemon balm, lavender, mints, rosemary, fennel, foxglove, thyme, hyssop, borage, chervil, clary, sage and costmary jostle in a silver-grey sea studded with nuggets of golden marigolds and old-fashioned wallflowers. Lady Salisbury's signature is recognized in the standard honeysuckles used as dot plants, which she introduced previously into the prodigious herb garden made in 1956 at her previous home *Cranborne Manor*, Dorset. While the Dorset garden is not on a site of ancient value (other than as a former burial ground!) it is not to be confused with a dainty knot garden set beneath library windows of the house at Cranborne. The herb garden is virtually a secret garden enclosed by cob wall and high yew hedge. Grass paths are frilled with cotton lavender and the whole garden set out for visual enjoyment.

At the American Museum in Britain, Claverton Manor, Bath, Avon, a traditional beehive is set at the centre of a tiny herb garden designed by Ian Mylles in 1964. (Photograph 1978)

Principal plants in the scented garden at Hatfield House mid-1970s		
Achillea decolorans	*Melissa officinalis*	'Leda'
Allium cepha	*Mentha × gentilis*	'Omar Khayyam'
Allium fistulosa	'Variegata'	*Rosa gallica*
Allium moly	*Mentha × piperita*	'Bell Isis'
Angelica archangelica	*Mentha spicata*	'Empress Joséphine'
Anthriscus cerefolium	*Mentha suaveolens*	'Hyppolyte'
Artemisia abrotanum	'Variegata'	'Jenny Duval'
Artemisia dracunculus	*Myrrhis odorata*	*Rosa gallica officinalis*
var. *sativa*	*Narcissus jonquilla*	'President de Sèze'
Artemisia schmidtiana	*Narcissus* 'White Sail'	'Tricolore de Flandre'
Borago officinalis	*Oenothera* sp.	'Tuscany Superb'
Calamintha grandiflora	*Origanum onites*	'Versicolor'
Calendula officinalis	*Originalum vulgare*	'*Rosa rubiginosa*
Cichorium intybus	'Aurea'	'Amy Robsart'
Chrysanthemum	*Polygonum bistorta*	'Meg Merrilies'
balsamita	*Poterium sanguisorba*	*Rosmarinus officinalis*
Cynara scolymus	*Primula* 'Gold Lace'	*Ruta graveolens*
Dianthus spp.	*Rosa alba*	*Tanacetum densum*
Digitalis purpurea	'Celestial'	*Tanacetum*
Foeniculum vulgare	'Maiden's Blush'	*fragrantissimum*
Helichrysum italicum	*Rosa centifolia*	*Thymus* sp.
Hyacinthus	'De Meaux'	*Tropaeolum majus*
'Salmonette'	'Juno'	*Tulipa batalinii* 'Bright
Hyssopus officinalis	*Rosa centifolia cristata*	Gem'
Iris reticulata 'J.S. Dijt'	(Chapeau de	*Tulipa clusiana*
Isatis tinctoria	Napoleon)	*Tulipa marjolettii*
Laurus nobilis	*Rosa centifolia muscosa*	*Tulipa stellata* var.
Lavandula spica	'Maréchal Davoust'	*chrysantha*
Levisticum officinalis	'Soupert et Notting'	*Tulipa* 'General de Wet'
Lonicera periclymenum	*Rosa damascena*	*Verbascum thapsiforme*
	'Celsiana'	

114

In front of the Old Palace at Hatfield House, Hertfordshire, the Marchioness of Salisbury has captured the historical importance of the site by laying a great knot garden in which plants of the Tudor period are grown. First the entire site was cleared and levelled, then measured and marked out in about 1980.

Two years later, the design was beginning to take form.

By the mid-1980s the whole scheme became evident and a remarkable collection of plants was assembled. Note the parterre maze.

Cotton lavender was chosen again by Lady Salisbury when she designed the first knot garden based on four 'Ts', for Tradescent, at the Museum of Garden History, St Mary-at-Lambeth, London. The Tradescants, father and son were seventeenth-century gardening giants responsible for introducing many plants into cultivation in England, and while the plants were not herbs a number of herb gardens have been made with seventeenth-century association, emphasizing maybe the period in which enthusiastic plantsmen ceased to eulogize over herbs, and ceased to cultivate them for decorative qualities.

One such, of considerable importance lies to one side of the Queen's Garden at *The Royal Botanic Gardens, Kew*, and is so rightly known as the Nosegay Garden. Here sit about 200 different species of plant known in the seventeenth century. Perhaps not every plant collected there is of economic value, nevertheless it affords a remarkable browsing and learning garden for the would-be herbarist, who may then rest on the chamomile seat!

Another garden with seventeenth-century associations is that set crisply regimented with New Court at Emmanual College, in the heart of Cambridge. Almost arresting in its simplicity, it was designed by John Codrington in 1961 based upon an early seventeenth-century design. Once again, trimmed box edging defines the skeleton of three separate triangular beds and smaller ones within each of them. As in Medieval days, each bed or section holds only one kind of plant, emphasizing the design by block planting. Other beds are embellished by coloured shale. The masterly touch on a somewhat awkward site is the two-colour paving which is laid in such a way as to disguise prospective.

Herb gardens and knot gardens, which we have come to accept as herb gardens by reason of their historical reference, are to be found in further locations with historical connotation. *Fulham Palace*, formerly the official residence of the Bishops of London, where the knot garden has been restored recently, is one example. Another is at the *Royal Botanic Garden, Edinburgh* where a physic garden was established in the seventeenth century, and at the University of Liverpool's *Botanic Garden at Ness*, Wirral where both a herb garden for the blind and the *Ledsham herb garden* laid out in 1974 can be enjoyed. The whole garden at Ness is noteworthy because it was first owned by a cotton broker, A. K. Bulley who sponsored plant-hunting expeditions about the turn of the twentieth century and who established the seed firm of Bees at Chester.

At *Chenies Manor*, Hertfordshire, part of the Woburn Estates of the Duke of Bedford, Mrs MacLeod Matthews has made a large physic garden which includes several less common physic plants and provides the background to some of the day courses organized at the Manor. Begun in 1976 the main borders are filled with culinary herbs and individual plots are devoted to plants yielding dyes, perfume and medicine. An amusing group of plants are labelled 'fallacies' — those which in the past were believed to have curative powers but have no proven value.

Let us not overlook a small herb border made by The National Trust in commemoration of Henry Lyte Esquire, the first amateur botanist to write a herbal, at his home *Lytes Cary Manor*, Somerset. In the house, a copy of *A Niewe Herball* (1578) is on display, and out in the garden the herb border is equally unsophisticated with lavender, artemisias, mints, rue and lilies.

Sometimes a dreamy nostalgia pervades many herb gardens, smudging the senses, so that the purist is distracted and the 'lavender and lace' brigade delighted. Happily both are catered for in the noteworthy garden at *The Welsh Folk Museum* (Amgueddfa Werin Cymru) at St Fagans Castle, Cardiff, South Wales. Not only are the plants labelled in Welsh, as is to be expected, but an accompanying booklet reveals a great deal of Welsh folk or fairy lore, spinning the visitor back to an ancient world in which these timeless plants were of immense value and importance.

Potager-style herb gardens

Un jardin potager is the French name for a kitchen garden, especially one laid out ornamentally to resemble a parterre. Usually it includes vegetables and fruit trees, the latter often grown in large pots. Herbs, especially pot herbs, play a considerable role in such a design reminiscent of Batty Langley's suggestions for a Gentleman's kitchen garden, as the National Trust has demonstrated at *Hardwick Hall*, Derbyshire; *Felbrigg*

Hall, Norfolk; *West Green House, Berkshire* and at *Gunby Hall*, Lincolnshire. The Trust's largest herb garden is that at Hardwick Hall, where the majority of herbs are culinary, and thus familiar. Designed by Paul Miles the garden falls into two identical parts connected by a central bed emphasized by wide gravel paths. About sixty culinary plants are assembled. At *West Green House*, fruit cages replicate charming flowery arbours across the garden and herbs mingle with the vegetables and tumble about the radial paths.

One of the most frequently visited *potager* is Rosemary Verey's at *Barnsley House, Gloucestershire* and a short distance away there is a border of herbs, the majority of which are culinary. Clipped box edging and finials contain the herb beds. Elsewhere there is a knot garden, formed mainly of box and germander. Thus in one garden *potager*, herbs and knot are enjoyed as separate features each displayed in simplicity.

Petersfield Physic Garden

It may seem surprising to find a seventeenth-century-style physic garden set in the heart of a bustling modern town, but in Petersfield, Hampshire, *The Hampshire Gardens Trust* has created a fascinating and carefully researched replica laid out very much in the style of the Chelsea Physic Garden and the Oxford Botanic Garden. Rectangular beds are arranged, in that period fashion, grid-like to allow inspection and ease of access. Innumerable herbs, culinary, medicinal, aromatic and economic have been assembled. Although the name physic garden was originally synonymous with botanic garden, it was during the seventeenth century that the distinction was made in England following the founding of these two famous gardens; 'physic' became associated with medicinal plants.

An eminent botanist at that time was John Goodyer who helped Johnson in the editing of Gerard's *Herball*. He lived and worked in Petersfield, and bequeathed his extensive library of botanical books and herbals to Magdalen College, Oxford. It seems appropriate, therefore, that the emblem chosen for the new physic garden should be the creeping lady's tresses orchid (*Goodyera repens*) which, although not a herb, commemorates the local association with John Goodyer.

The garden is within a walled garden on a site donated by Major J. C. E. Bowen in 1988 to The Hampshire Gardens Trust to be maintained for education and enjoyment. The long rectangular site has, it is believed, been cultivated since the twelfth century and it was Major Bowen's intention that it should continue so, rather than fall into the hands of developers. To complement the formal beds of economic herbs there is an orchard of seventeenth-century apple varieties, such as 'Nonpareil', 'Cornish Aromatic' and 'Devonshire Quarrenden'; medlars, quinces and the pear 'Catillac'; beds of flowering perennials known in the period, such as *Hemerocallis flava, Campanula glomerata, Veronica spicata, Pulsatilla vulgaris, Geranium phaeum, Lobelia syphilitica*, some florists' flowers and many more. At the far end a bed of roses of the period has been designed by that much respected rosarian, Hazel le Rougetel and she has included *gallica* forms, centifolias and *R. eglanteria*, and on the wall to festoon the background such lovely favourites as the York and Lancaster rose (*R. damascena*) and *R. d.* 'Quatre Saisons' and *R. alba semiplena*. Wild flowers have not been overlooked, and the emphasis is on some endangered species.

A competition was held to design a suitable knot garden, and the winning design was planted in late 1990. Remarkably it echoes that which forms part of the family coat of arms of Major Bowen, and was designed by Mrs Joanne Allen, an amateur designer. Slightly adapted, as far as planting was concerned the defining square is outlined by santolina, and softened by dianthus and the central knot is formed in box. No more than five herbs are used in the design; lavender, germander, dianthus, together with the box and santolina, which makes a bold and clear statement.

The William Ransom Physic Garden

The market town of Hitchin in Hertfordshire is still known today after more than a century and a half as the home of William Ransom and Son, manufacturing pharmacists. To honour the founder, the *William Ransom Physic Garden* has been laid out on a small plot adjoining the Hitchin Museum, Paynes Park in the centre of the town. Opened in May 1990 by Professor Harold Ellis of the Department of Clinical Anatomy, University of Cambridge, the garden is enclosed by fine Victorian-style iron railings so that the passing public can share their pride.

At the centre of this enchanting little garden is a pedestal carrying a pharmacist's pestle and mortar in metal with the inscription around the inside rim: 'Disease does oft rise above medicine. W. M. Drage 1632–1668. A Hitchin Apothecary.' On the outside of the pestle we are told that it is In Memoriam: Mr D. W. Jimmy James, late President and Dr Douglas Willet, late Vice President, the Hertfordshire Medical and Pharmaceutical Trust. The garden is an irregular hexagonal in shape and the herbs are collected in beds according to their uses, each being labelled by name and a quotation from Gerard or Parkinson added. Deidre Boggon researched and designed the garden.

The enterprise extends further in that inside the Hitchin Museum, a Victorian chemist's shop has been reconstructed. Perhaps 'reconstructed' is not quite the correct word for many of the fittings were preserved by Miss Violet Lewis, herself a pharmacist, when her chemist's shop was sold for the development of a modern Woolworths in 1961. She harboured stock and equipment and continued to augment her collection and has now transferred it to the safe keeping of the Hertfordshire Medical and Pharmaceutical Trust (HMPMT). Funds for this and the herb garden were accrued from local firms and individuals, William Ransom and Son and the Hitchin District Council. An enthusiastic working party takes credit for the assembling of the shop.

Mahogany counters and shining glass-fronted cupboards loaded with bottles and packets and bygone preparations all deemed necessities in their day, recreate the appearance and atmosphere evocative of a Victorian shop, but it is the display of lavender products that offers the key to the story of that other lavender growing enterprise in Hitchin. Shaving soap, smelling salts, dentrifice, soaps, face and talcum powders, lavender water, bath salts, sachets and an array of packaging, much of it tinted a delicate mauve each recall a past age. Consequently the Museum now does a good line in souvenirs in the form of lavender flowers and stalks woven with mauve ribbon into little bottle-shaped 'dollies' or faggots.

Work began on the Queen's Garden at the Royal Botanic Garden, Kew in 1963 to form a plot representative of seventeenth-century plants. It was opened by H M The Queen in May 1969. (Photograph 1980)

Present-day lavender growing

Harvesting of lavender takes place in mid- and late summer in England, varying perhaps a week or two according to the weather. As with all herbs, the cutting time is critical, not only because the small flowers will drop if left too long but because the maximum of essential oil must be harvested. The oil accumulates in tiny sacs, at the base of each flower and the amount depends upon warmth and sunshine while the flowers are blooming.

Waving acres of lavender flowers in northern East Anglia centre around the little town of Heacham. The headquarters of the enterprise, the Norfolk Lavender Company is at Coley Mill, the stronghold of Henry Head. Now the farm is the home of the National Collection of Lavenders in addition to being the largest commercial lavender enterprise in the UK. No longer do sunburned women reap the harvest with sickle-like lavender knives, because since the mid-1960s a machine combs in the flower spikes to chop them evenly from the plant, creating great swathes across the fields, and conveys them aloft to sacks. So, direct from field to distillery they go with a minimum of delay. There they are tumbled out in piles, forked into one of the large copper stills, trampled and distilled. The precious oil of lavender soon oozes through, just an hour or two after the spikes were cut.

Much of the oil goes to Yardley Ltd and has done since the mid-1930s when stills were installed on site to avoid the delay of transporting cut lavender to Suffolk for oil extraction. Amid the hazy blue fields of high summer crisply scented products are sold in the Company's shop — products such as soap, toiletries, perfume, sachets and dried lavender spikes just as have been used, albeit in a less sophisticated form, for centuries.

Disaster threatened during the 1960s when shab disease devastated the crop, but a Yardley director travelled the world to locate and introduce new disease-resistant strains. Experiment and expansion continues, to assure the high quality of the typical fresh aroma of Norfolk-cultivated lavender.

The Main Garden at Hardwick Hall, Derbyshire is divided into compartments by yew and hornbeam hedges. Within one square the National Trust laid out a potager style herb garden in the early 1970's designed by Paul Miles. The herb garden itself is again set in four squares, punctured by posts that support golden leaved hops. (Photograph 1980)

NEW WORLD TAPESTRY AND HERBS

What we are asked to contemplate in a modern tapestry currently being created in the West Country are some of the events, places and people that were involved in the colonizing of North America. The voluntary project is the hobby and brainchild of Plymouth artist Tom Mor who has designed 23 panels, each 3.5 m (11 ft) wide and 1.2 m (4 ft) deep, which when assembled will represent a caricature reportage of the years 1583–1642. Leading emigrant families and their companions and the American Indians are the chief actors in this parade, coats of arms proclaim their status in the home country and the herbs they used provide the historic link between the two continents. Tom Mor is quick to acknowledge the help in researching history and heraldry from Tom Maddock, one time Mayor of Ivybridge and Paul Presswell of Buckfastleigh, and for herbs from Freda Simpson, herself the grand-daughter of a locally well-known herbalist in Launceston, Cornwall.

In design the herbs are symbolized reminiscent in style of an earlier period with which the players in this tableau would have been familiar from old herbals. When assembled the entire upper and lower borders will be formed of herbs, providing an outstanding catalogue of plant history. The settlers took with them, as companions, copies of Gerard's, Parkinson's and Culpeper's herbals and such identifiable influences as these men are depicted in the final 1642 panel of the tapestry together with intriguing references to John Tradescant and some of the American plants with which he was associated. At the centre of this panel is a plan of the Oxford Botanic Garden which, as we have seen, was the first to be founded in England in 1621.

Brightly coloured, the tapestry has a clear educational value and yet amusement is provided by the cartoon approach with which both young and old can identify. When complete it is estimated that the entire length will manifest well over 37 300 000 stitches each lovingly made by either volunteer embroiderers or patrons. Upon payment of £1, I made my one stitch (and received a little certificate to verify that it was part of the tare (*Vicia* sp.). Her Majesty The Queen and the Duke of Edinburgh each made their own stitch during the Armada celebrations at HMS Drake at Devonport in 1988. Volunteer embroiderers have worked over the past 15 years at nine centres throughout Devon and Dorset and now work at five main centres; Plymouth, Exeter, Bideford, Lyme Regis and Tiverton. Honorary Patrons include the governors of some of the New England States and the US Ambassador to London in addition to eminent people in England binding the whole project, which began in 1975 to record the historical data which in many respects enriched the medicine chests and the gardens of both continents.

Worked entirely in tent stitch, or oblique Gobelin stitch, 16 stitches to the inch in wool generously donated by Emu Wool, it is planned to exhibit four or five of the 23 panels in Tiverton, Devon during 1991. At Nomansland about eight miles from Tiverton an Elizabethan style garden features more than 150 of the 253 herbs depicted on the tapestry, those that John Josselyn had listed together with many described by Gerard, Parkinson and known to Culpeper. Members of the public who visited the exhibition in 1991 may have seen the final 1642 panel being sewn to complete the entire project.

PLANT CONSERVATION

During the nineteenth and early twentieth centuries, with heightened activity to produce spectacular cultivars, herbs escaped the hybridists' attention. Modesty has ensured their survival. Further, during the past 30 years the increased demand has meant that plant nurseries and propagators have been encouraged to track down many herbs that were falling out of cultivation, in order to meet the commercial demand. Thus, unwittingly and totally unintentionally a most forceful conservation exercise has been accomplished. Today, read any reputable establishment's herb catalogue and included there will be plants that a generation ago were virtually unavailable commercially.

National Council for the Conservation of Plants and Gardens

In 1978 the NCCPG was formed under the auspices of the Royal Horticultural Society. Broadly speaking the brief was to ensure the safety of many garden plants that were seriously threatened and probably likely to fall out of cultivation, or at least become commercially unavailable. Part of the action taken has been to establish National Collections — well over 500 in the first decade — of plants which will serve as stock material. Several Collections include herbs but there is no National Collection of herbs *per se* because Collections are assembled on a generic basis. Thus the official plant will be but one example, within a Collection, probably accompanied by its various forms and cultivars (see page 126).

BACK TO WILD FLOWERS

Today it is estimated that there are about a hundred commercial outlets in the UK from which the would-be herb gardener can obtain plants apart from markets and garden centres. In addition the seedsmen offer an ever-increasing range of herbs and cultivar forms. Developing interest in wild flower gardening during the 1980s has resulted in several farms being established for the production of wild-flower seed, and seed mixtures. John Chambers Wild Flower Seeds from Kettering, Northamptonshire is widely known and in the popular mind was the pioneer nursery offering seed more than ten years ago. The name of Suffolk Herbs at Sudbury, Suffolk is also well to the fore augmented by unusual salad herbs and vegetables.

A recent wild flower enterprise is being established on a windy cliff site at Osmington in Dorset. About forty varying mixtures for streamside, boggy meadow, heathland, calcareous or clay soil and other natural habitats are composed at Heritage Seeds. David Russell has developed the mixtures, some comprising as many as 20–30 species according to the data bank information he and his wife have developed. Although over 220 plants are already plotted, they believe they will extend to some 600 varieties. Starting with seed collecting from the wild, and taking no more than two subsequent crops before returning to collect afresh from the wild they are involved in a labour-intensive but intriguing process, so that now a Medieval flowery mead can be replicated or a Victorian meadow or cornfield verge from which the country women collected the ingredients for their herbal remedies.

The flowery mead

Since the Conservation of Wild Creatures and Wild Plants Act of 1975, the public at large and landowners in particular have at least been aware of the intrinsic value of many wild plants. The Medieval flowery mead represented the simplest form of cultivation and wild flowers and, it must be remembered, were the herbs of Chaucer's time, the plants Gerard and his associates used, and the objects of Johnson's herborizing parties. Wild flowers tempted the Victorians on to the newly sibilant trains to indulge in field forays and assemble herbaria. Twentieth-century 'progress' has sprayed verges and meadows with plant poisons and soused them with nitrates, made silage for cows rather than hay, which necessitates cutting before plants flower. All of which has obliterated nature's herbs. Some credit must be due to the herb growers, both commercial and amateur for conserving some of the wild plants that boast such a steadfast history. We can only trust that sanity will prevail as science hurtles towards other worlds and other centuries.

Whither herbs?

Now that this remarkable plant conservation exercise has been accomplished it seems that the sensual appeal of the herb garden overrides that of tradition. The flowery mead is accepted, experimental although it remains in some instances, as the oldest and simplest form of gardening — a meadow spattered with flowers. The grander herb gardens of the past three decades have tended to become scented or nosegay gardens probably because the green aromatics themselves display a comparatively short season of interest, starting late and 'going over' as the gardener says, once seed has set in late summer.

An up-dated theme of the all-purpose garden of the peasants of the great and general past, where in a lighthearted manner all economic plants claim equality, is a *potager*. Without doubt, the *potager* is gaining in popularity in domestic garden design,

The Petersfield Physic Garden, constructed by members of the Hampshire Gardens Trust is still being made along seventeenth century physic garden lines. It offers an example of local generosity and effort to prevent development and to create instead a token to our botanical heritage.

especially where land is at a premium and the multitude of herbs will find their place there. Maximum formality often based on Medieval rectangular beds ranged in rows, or modernized to emulate the Union Jack with radiating pathways, the *potager* is decorated with an abundance of economic plants, colourful vegetables, herbs and modern compact fruit tree forms — the modern garden for a modern classless society.

As with all garden styles the moment of completion never comes. Maybe there is an evening when the afterglow of a summer day throws theatrical lights and shadows across the garden, and the gardener himself senses the completion, but the living burgeoning art form needs constant adaption and personal attention. Similarly, with garden style: how do we identify the moment from history when modern herb gardens had their inception? Gardeners of the past drew ideas from their forebears to interpret as their own.

Yet, it seems that *a period* in garden history is expressed in the formal herb garden, a period when the plant world paused. The Paradise garden enclosed, protected with water representing the fount of life, was a comparatively recent memory and therefore understood. New and exciting plant introductions motivated the study of both botany and horticulture, the tried and tested plants that needed little cultural knowledge remained — those we call herbs. At the parting of the ways, the Stuarts were ironing out the frivolities of Tudor taste. Knot gardens represented a playful garden challenge and it seemed 'sensible' to contemporary taste to simplify them by spreading the component sections as beds, each outlined in box to form the new-fashioned parterre. John Parkinson advocated 'the fairer and larger your alles and walkes be, the more grace your garden will have, the less harme the herbes and flowers shall receive by passing by them that grow next unto the allies sides . . .'. He was differentiating already between herbs and flowers; the aesthetic intent was an innovation in gardening.

No actual authority emerges for herb garden design or style; we built only upon a period — a period in which herbs were left in domestic plots, their survival dependent upon their service to man, their genetics ignored by generations to come. Today we collect and cultivate them in much the same way as did gardeners of the Tudor and Stuart periods, pouncing upon a red-leaved or double-flowered form, or selecting a better flavoured or less rampant kind, and we have set them in parterre-like patterns of that period to honour them as aesthetically desirable plants every bit as interesting as the outlandish plants that outstripped them 300 years ago.

Maybe formal decorative herb gardens are museum pieces after all! Old plants in new gardens, and yet, the plants carry the secrets of olden wisdom bound in gossamer threads of past evolutions.

BIBLIOGRAPHY

Amherst, Alicia. *A History of Gardening in England*, 3rd edn, John Murray, 1909.

Arber, Agnes. *Herbals, their Origin and Evolution 1470–1670*, Cambridge University Press, 1912.

Bardswell, Frances A. *The Herb Garden*, A & C Black, 1911.

Brownlow, Margaret E. *Herbs and the Fragrant Garden*, The Herb Farm, 1957.

Brownlow, Margaret E. *The Delights of Herb Growing*, The Herb Farm, 1964.

Clapham, A R., Tutin, T. G., and Warburg, E. F. *Flora of the British Isles*, Cambridge University Press, 1952.

Culpeper, N. *The English Physician enlarged with Three Hundred and Sixty-nine Medicines made of English Herbs*, 1775.

Day, Ivan. *Perfumery with Herbs*, Darton, Longman & Todd, 1979.

Dutton, Ralph. *The English Garden*, B. T. Batsford, 1937.

Fairbrother, Nan. *Men and Gardens*, Hogarth Press, 1956.

Festing, Sally. *The Story of Lavender*, London Borough of Sutton Libraries and Arts Service, 1982.

Gloag, M. R. *A Book of British Gardens*, 1906.

Gordon, Lesley. *Green Magic*, Ebury Press, 1977.

Grieve, Maud. *A Modern Herbal*, Jonathan Cape, 1934.

Griggs, Barbara. *Green Pharmacy*, Jill Norman & Hobhouse, 1981.

Harvey, John. *Early Gardening Catalogues*, Phillimore, 1981.

Harvey, John. *Medieval Gardens*, B. T. Batsford, 1981.

Henrey, Blanche. *British Botanical and Horticultural Literature before 1800*, Vol. 1, Henrey, Oxford University Press, 1975.

Hewer, Dorothy and Sanecki, Kay N. *Practical Herb Growing*, Geo. Bell, 1968.

Lehane, Brendan. *The Power of Plants*, John Murray, 1977.

McLintock, David. *Companion to Flowers*, Geo. Bell, 1966.

Rohde, Eleanour Sinclair. *A Garden of Herbs*, Medici Society, 1920.

Rohde, Eleanour Sinclair. *Herbs and Herb Gardening*, Medici Society, 1936.

Rohde, Eleanour Sinclair. *The Old English Herbals*, Minerva Press, 1974.

Sanecki, Kay N. *Wild and Garden Herbs*, Collingridge, 1956.

Sanecki, Kay N. *The Complete Book of Herbs*, MacDonald, 1974.

Strabo, Walahfrid. *Hortulus*, transl. Raef Payne, Hunt Botanical Library, Philadelphia, 1966.

Stuart, Malcolm, ed. *Encyclopedia of Herbs and Herbalism*, Orbis, 1979.

Teetgen, Ada T. *Profitable Herb Growing and Collecting*, Country Life, 1916.

Thomson, William A. R., ed. *Healing Plants, A Modern Herbal*, Macmillan, 1978.

Tusser, Thomas. *Four Hundred Points of Good Husbandrie*, 1557.

Weeks, Nora. *The Medical Discoveries of Edward Bach*, C. W. Daniel.

Wheelwright, Edith Grey. *The Physic Garden*, Jonathan Cape, 1934.

Wilson, C. Anne. *Food and Drink in Britain*, Penguin, 1973.

Woodward, Marcus ed. *Gerard's Herbal* (Johnson Edition), Studio Editions, 1979.

Journal of The Royal Horticultural Society.

APPENDIX I

PLANTS MENTIONED IN THE TEXT

Absinth *Artemisia absinthium*
Adder's tongue *Ophioglossum vulgatum*
Agrimony *Agrimonia eupatoria*
Alexanders *Smyrnium olusatrum*
Alkanet *Pentaglottis sempervirens*
Angelica *Angelica archangelica*
Anise *Pimpinella anisum*
Arum *Arum maculatum*
Bay *Laurus nobilis*
Bean, broad *Vicia faba*
Bearberry *Arctostaphylos uve-ursi*
Belladonna *Atropa belladonna*
Betony *Stachys officinalis*
Borage *Boraga officinalis*
Box *Buxus sempervirens*
Bryony *Bryonia dioica*
Bugle *Ajuga reptans*
Bugloss *Lycopsis arvensis*
Burnet saxifrage *Pimpinella saxifraga*
Calamint *Calamintha ascendens*
Caraway *Carum carvi*
Catmint *Nepeta cataria*
Celandine *Ranunculus ficaria*
Celery *Apium graveolens*
Centaury *Centaurium minus*
Chamomile *Chaemamelum nobile*
Chervil *Anthriscus cerefolium*
Chicory *Cichorium intybus*
Chives *Allium schoenoprasum*
Christmas rose *Helleborus niger*
Clary *Salvia sclarea*
Colchicum *Colchicum autumnale*
Colewort *Brassica oleracea*
Coltsfoot *Tussilago farfara*
Columbine *Aquilegia vulgaris*
Comfrey *Symphytum officinale*
Coriander *Coriandrum sativum*
Costmary, alecost *Chrysanthemum balsamita*
Cotton lavender *Santolina chamaecyparissus*
Cowslip *Primula veris*
Cress *Lepidium sativum*
Cucumber *Cucumis sativus*
Cumin *Cuminum cyminum*
Daffodil *Narcissus pseudonarcissus*
Daisy *Bellis perennis*
Dame's violet *Hesperis matronalis*
Dandelion *Taraxacum officinale*
Dittany *Origanum dictamnus*
Dodder *Cuscuta epithymum*
Elder *Sambucus nigra*
Elecampane *Inula helenium*
Endive *Cichorium endiva*
Eyebright *Euphrasia officinale*
Fennel *Foeniculum vulgare*
Fenugreek *Trigonella foenum-graecum*
Feverfew *Chrysanthemum parthenium*
Fig *Ficus carica*
Flax *Linum usitatissimum*

Fleabane *Erigeron canadense*
Foxglove *Digitalis purpurea*
Gentian *Gentiana lutea*
Germander *Teucrium chamaedrys*
Gillyflower *Dianthus* sp. and *Cheiranthus* spp.
Gipsywort *Lycopus europaeus*
Ground ivy *Glechoma hederacea*
Hellebore, black *Helleborsus niger*
Hellebore, green *Veratrum viride*
Hellebore, white *Veratrum alba*
Hemp *Cannabis sativa*
Hellebore, black *Helleborus niger*
Herb patience *Rumex patientia*
Holly *Ilex aquifolium*
Hollyhock *Althaea rosea*
Honeysuckle *Lonicera periclymenum*
Hop *Humulus lupulus*
Horehound, black *Ballota nigra*
Horehound, white *Marrubium vulgare*
Horseradish *Cochlearia armoracia*
Horsetail *Equisetum arvensis*
Houseleek *Sempervivum tectorum*
Hyssop *Hyssopus officinalis*
Iris, purple *Iris garmanica*
Iris, white *Iris florentina*
Iris, yellow *Iris pseudacorus*
Jacob's ladder *Polemonium caeruleum*
Juniper *Juniperus communis*
Lady's bedstraw *Galium verum*
Langue de bouef *Picris echioides*
Lavender *Lavandula angustifolia*
Lemon balm *Melissa officinalis*
Lettuce *Lactuca sativa*
Licorice *Glycyrrhiza glabra*
Lily, madonna *Lilium candidum*
Lily-of-the-valley *Convallaria majalis*
Lovage *Levisticum officinale*
Lungwort *Pulmonaria officinalis*
Madder *Rubia tinctorum*
Mallow *Malva sylvestris*
Mandrake *Mandragora officinarum*
Marigold *Calendula officinalis*
Marjoram *Origanum vulgare*
Marshmallow *Althaea officinalis*
Meadowsweet *Filipendula ulmaria*
Medlar *Mesphilis germanica*
Melon *Cucumis melo*
Mint *Mentha* spp.
Monkshood *Aconitum napellus*
Motherwort *Leonorus cardiaca*
Mugwort *Artemisia vulgaris*
Mullein *Verbascum thapsus*
Nettle *Urtica dioica*
Nightshade, black *Solanum nigrum*
Nightshade, deadly *Atropa belladonna*
Orach *Atriplex hortensis*
Orpine *Sedum telephinum*
Orris *Iris florentina*
Paeony *Paeonia officinalis*
Parsley *Petroselenum crispum*
Parsnip *Peucedanum sativum*
Pea *Pisum sativum*

Pennyroyal *Mentha pulegium*
Periwinkle *Vinca major*
Pimpernel *Anagalis arvensis*
Pink *Dianthus caryophyllus*
Plantain *Plantago minor*
Plantain, waybread *Plantago major*
Poppy *Papaver somniferum*
Poppy, field *Papaver rhoeas*
Primrose *Primula vulgaris*
Purslane *Portulaca oleracea*
Quince *Cydonia oblonga*
Ragged Robin *Lychnis flos-cucculi*
Ragwort *Senecio jacobaea*
Ramsons *Allium ursinum*
Raspberry *Rubus idaeus*
Rocket *Eruca sativa*
Rocket, sweet *Hesperis matronalis*
Rose *Rosa gallica*
Rosemary *Rosmarinus officinalis*
Rue *Ruta graveolens*
Saffron *Crocus sativus*
Sage *Salvia officinalis*
St John's wort *Hypericum perforatum*
Salad burnet *Poterium sanguisorba*
Samphire *Salicornia* spp.
Savory, summer *Satureia hortensis*
Savory, winter *Satureia montana*
Scabious *Knautia arvensis*
Scabwort *Inula helenium*
Sea holly *Eryngium maritima*
Selfheal *Prunella vulgaris*
Snowflake *Leucojum aestivum*
Soapwort *Saponaria officinalis*
Solomon's seal *Polygonatum multiflorum*
Southernwood *Artemisia abrotanum*
Strawberry, wild *Fragaria vesca*
Sweet Cicely *Myrrhis odorata*
Sweet William *Dianthus barbatus*
Tansy *Chrysanthemum tanacetum*
Teazel *Dipsacus fullonum*
Thyme *Thymus vulgaris*
Thyme, wild *Thymus serpyllum*
Valerian *Valeriana officinalis*
Vine *Vitis vinifera*
Violet *Viola odorata*
Wallflower *Cheiranthus cheiri*
Walnut *Juglans nigra*
Watercress *Nasturtium -aquaticum*
Waterlily *Nymphaea alba*
Winter cherry *Physalis alkekengii*
Woad *Isatis tinctoria*
Woodruff *Gallium odoratum* (Syn. *Asperula odorata*)
Wood sage *Teucrium scorodonia*
Wood sorrel *Oxalis acetosella*
Wormwood *Artemisia absinthium*
Yarrow *Achillea millefolium*
Yellow flag *Iris pseudacorus*
Yew *Taxus baccata*

APPENDIX II
WHERE OUR HERBS CAME FROM

Many of our herbs are British native plants, or at least Northern Europe natives. Others come from Southern Europe and countries bordering the Mediterranean; some were introduced by the Romans, some were reintroduced later, others arrived during the fifteenth and sixteenth centuries. Later, after the opening up of the New World, others came from the North American continent, although their arrival was somewhat overshadowed by the wide range of decorative plants which captured the attention of gardeners.

BRITISH NATIVES

In many instances native plants and well-established introduced plants are hard to distinguish. The following are the principal herbs considered to be British.

Absinth	*Artemisia absinthium*
Adder's tongue	*Ophioglossum vulgatum*
Agrimony	*Agrimonia eupatoria*
Arum	*Arum maculatum*
Bearberry	*Arctostaphylos uva-ursi*
Belladonna	*Atropa belladonna*
Betony	*Stachys officinalis*
Box	*Buxus sempervirens*
Bryony	*Bryonia dioica*
Bugle	*Ajuga reptans*
Bugloss	*Lycopsis arvensis*
Burdock	*Arctum lappa*
Burnet saxifrage	*Pimpinella saxifraga*
Calamint	*Calamintha ascendens*
Catmint	*Nepeta cataria*
Celandine	*Ranunculus ficaria*
Celery	*Apium graveolens*
Centaury	*Centaurium minus*
Chamomile	*Chamaemelum nobile*
Chicory	*Cichorium intybus*
Chives	*Allium schoenoprasum*
Christmas rose	*Helleborus niger*
Clary	*Salvia sclarea*
Colchicum	*Colchicum autumnale*
Coltsfoot	*Tussilago farfara*
Columbine	*Aquilegia vulgaris*
Comfrey	*Symphytum officinale*
Cowslip	*Primula veris*
Cress	*Lepidium sativum*
Daisy	*Bellis perennis*
Dandelion	*Taraxacum officinalis*
Elder	*Sambucus nigra*
Eyebright	*Euphrasia officinale*
Feverfew	*Chrysanthemum parthenium*
Fleabane	*Erigeron canadense*
Foxglove	*Digitalis purpurea*
Gipsywort	*Lycopus europaeus*
Ground ivy	*Glechoma hederacea*
Heartsease	*Viola tricolor*
Hellebore, black	*Helleborus niger*
Henbane	*Hyoscyamus niger*
Holly	*Ilex aquifolium*
Hop	*Humulus lupulus*
Horehound, black	*Ballota nigra*
Horehound, white	*Marrubium vulgare*
Horsetail	*Equisetum arvensis*
Iris, yellow	*Iris pseudacorus*
Jacob's ladder	*Polemonium caeruleum*
Juniper	*Juniperus communis*
Lady's bedstraw	*Galium verum*
Lily-of-the-valley	*Convallaria majalis*
Lime tree	*Tilea europea*
Lovage	*Levisticum officinale*
Lungwort	*Pulmonaria officinalis*
Mallow	*Malva sylvestris*
Marjoram	*Origanum vulgare*
Marshmallow	*Althaea officinalis*
Meadowsweet	*Filipendula ulmaria*
Mint, corn	*Mentha arvensis*
Mint, water	*Mentha aquatica*
Monkshood	*Aconitum napellus*
Mugwort	*Artemisia vulgare*
Mullein	*Verbascum thapsus*
Nettle	*Urtica dioica*
Nightshade, black	*Solanum nigrum*
Nightshade, deadly	*Atropa belladonna*
Orpine	*Sedum telephinum*
Parsnip	*Peucedanum sativum*
Pennyroyal	*Mentha pulegium*
Pimpernel	*Anagalis arvensis*
Pink	*Dianthus caryophyllus*
Plantain	*Plantago major*
Poppy, field	*Papaver rhoeas*
Primrose	*Primula vulgaris*
Ragwort	*Senecio jacobaea*
Ramsons	*Allium ursinum*
Raspberry	*Rubus idaeus*
St John's wort	*Hypericum perforatum*
Samphire	*Salicornia* spp.
Sea holly	*Eryngium maritimum*
Selfheal	*Prunella vulgaris*
Soapwort	*Saponaria officinalis*
Solomon's seal	*Polygonatum multiflorum*
Strawberry, wild	*Fragaria vesca*
Sweet Cicely	*Myrrhis odorata*
Tansy	*Chrysanthemum tanacetum*
Teazel	*Dipsacus fullonum*
Thyme, wild	*Thymus serpyllum*
Valerian	*Valeriana officinalis*
Vervain	*Verbena officinalis*
Violet	*Viola odorata*
Watercress	*Nasturtium-aquaticum*
Woad	*Isatis tinctoria*
Woodruff	*Gallium odoratum* (syn. *Asperula odoratum*)
Wood sage	*Teucrium scordonia*
Wood sorrel	*Oxalis acetosella*
Wormwood	*Artemisia absinthium*
Yarrow	*Achillea millefolium*
Yellow flag	*Iris pseudacorus*

HERBS FROM SOUTHERN EUROPE AND COUNTRIES BORDERING THE MEDITERRANEAN

Alkanet	*Pentaglottis sempervirens*
Anise	*Pimpinella anisum*
Borage	*Borago officinalis*
Caraway	*Carum carvi*
Chervil	*Anthriscus cerefolium*
Coriander	*Coriandrum sativum*
Elecampane	*Inula helenium*
Fenugreek	*Trigonella foenum-graecum*
Gentian	*Gentiana lutea*
Iris, purple	*Iris germanica*
Iris, white	*Iris florentina*
Lavender	*Lavandula angustifolia*
Lemon Balm	*Melissa officinalis*
Marjoram, pot	*Origanum onites*
Marjoram, sweet	*Origanum majorana*
Paeony	*Paeonia officinalis*
Rosemary	*Rosmarinus officinalis*
Savory, summer	*Satureia hortensis*
Savory, winter	*Satureia montana*
Southernwood	*Artemisia abrotanum*
Thyme	*Thymus vulgaris*

HERBS FROM NORTH AMERICA

Abcessroot	*Polmarium reptans*	Jessamine, yellow	*Gelsemium sempervirens*	Scullcap, Virginian	*Scutelaria laterifolia*
Balm	*Monarda didyma*	Labrador tea	*Ledum latifolium*	Snakeroot	*Polygola senega*
Bloodroot	*Leptandra virginica*	Mandrake,		Snakeroot, black	*Cimifuga racemosa*
Coral root,	*Cotallorhiza odontorhiza*	American	*Podophyllum peltatum*	Stoneroot	*Collinsonia canadensis*
Crawley root	*Cotallorhiza odontorhiza*	Mayapple	*Podophyllum peltatum*	Wild senna	*Cassia marylandica*
Evening primrose	*Oenothera biennis*	Pleurisy root	*Asclepias tuberosa*	Wintergreen	*Gaultheria procumbens*
Fleabane	*Erigeron canadensis*	Pokeroot	*Phytolacca americana*	Witch hazel	*Hamamelis virginiana*
Hellebore, green	*Veratrum viride*	Pukeweed	*Lobelia inflata*	Wormgrass	*Spigelia marylandica*
Indian physic	*Gillenia trifoliata*	Red root	*Ceanothus americanus*	Wormseed	*Chenopodium*
Indian poke	*Veratrum viride*	Sarsaparilla	*Aralia nudicaulis*		*anthelminticum*
Indigo, wild	*Baptisia tinctoria*	Sassafras	*Sassafras officinalis*	Yellow root	*Hydrastis canadensis*

APPENDIX III
NATIONAL COLLECTIONS

Boragio (borage)
Scotia Pharmaceuticals Ltd
Scotia Plant Research Unit
Writtle Agricultural College
Chelmsford, Essex CM1 3RR

Calamintha
Mrs L. M. Williams
Marle Place
Brenchley
Kent TN12 7HS

Eryngium
Mr J. Lamont
Lancashire College of Agriculture &
    Horticulture
Myerscough Hall, Billsbarrow
Preston, Lancashire PR3 0RY

Lavandula
Mr David Christie
Jersey Lavender Ltd
Rue Dupont, Marquet St Brelade,
Jersey, Channel Isles

Mr Henry Head
Norfolk Lavender Ltd
Heacham
Norfolk PE31 7JE

Mentha
Mr R. Lunn
Herbs in Stock
White Hill, Stock
Ingatestone, Essex.

Monarda
Mr Maurice Bristow
Leeds Castle
Nr Maidstone, Kent ME17 1PL

Nepeta
Mr Maurice Bristow
Leeds Castle
Nr Maidstone, Kent ME17 1PL

Pulmonaria
Mrs Vanessa Cook
Stillingfleet Lodge Nursery
Stillingfleet, York YO4 6HW

Rheum
The Curator
Harlow Carr Botanic Gardens
Crag Lane, Harrogate
N. Yorkshire H93 1QB

Rosmarinus
Messrs R & M Cheek
35 Wimbledon Rise
Bridgwater
Somerset

Salvia
Mr R. Wadey
Dorset College of
    Agriculture
Kingston Maurward
Dorchester
Dorset DT2 8PY

Santolina
Mrs L. M. Williams
Marle Place
Benchley, Kent
TN12 7HS

Tanacetum
Mr G. W. Goddard
25 Mornington Road
Chingford
London E4 7DJ

Thymus
Mr & Mrs F. Huntington
Quantock Herbs
Hethersett
Cothelstone
Taunton
Somerset TD4 3DP

Mr K. A. White
Hexham Herbs
Chesters Walled Garden
Chollerford, Hexham
Northumberland

INDEX